MEDITATIONS FOR R

TAKEN FROM THE WRITINGS OF

ST. FRANCIS DE SALES.

ARRANGED BY

ST. JANE FRANCES FRÉMIOT DE CHANTAL.

FROM THE FRENCH

BY A VISITANDINE OF BALTIMORE

A Book of Meditation Retreat Contemplations
from the Writing Of Holy St Francis de Sales
on God, Providence, Heaven and Love of Neighbor

Affinity Imprints, 2022

NEW YORK, CINCINNATI, CHICAGO:
BENZIGER BROTHERS,
Printers to the Holy Apostolic See.
1900.

Nihil Obstat.

REMY LAFORT,
Censor Librorum.

Imprimatur:

✛ MICHAEL AUGUSTINE,
Archbishop of New York.

NEW YORK, January 16, 1900.

Copyright, 1900, by BENZIGER BROTHERS.

Mother de Chantal to the Sisters of the Visitation.

My very dear Sisters:

We gladly send you this manuscript, as it is taken from the works of our blessed Father, and especially from several memoirs written by his dear and holy hand. These are his thoughts and words; you will readily recognize in them his spirit. We have endeavored to abridge and arrange them into Meditations that may serve for the retreats made before the renovation of our vows, because many of our Sisters, the Superioresses, have long urged us to do so. I think that, after the first and second parts of Philothea, you will find nothing more solid or practical. If you read and reflect upon them attentively, they will enlighten your understanding and inflame your hearts. The Meditations on Silence, on Modesty, and on several other religious virtues are wanting, because these subjects were not treated in the brief memoirs of our blessed Father. You will find them in the exercises of Reverend Father Dom Sens, which our blessed Father held in great esteem, or elsewhere. Believe me, my very dear Sisters, I most cheerfully communicate to you all that we possess of the writings of our holy Founder, being anxious beyond expression that we may live upon his sweet and holy doctrine. May God grant us the grace to accomplish this! Supplicate His goodness in behalf of

Your unworthy Sister and servant in Our Lord,

Sister JANE FRANCES FRÉMIOT.

God be praised! Amen.

Preface.

It is a custom observed from time immemorial among the children of God, who knows the frailty and weakness of their nature, to renew their good purposes and holy resolutions. The Israelites, the chosen people of God, did so at every new moon, when the trumpet was sounded, and a solemn festival held, in order to elevate the mind to eternal things. Holy Church, from time to time, presents grand feasts and solemnities to her children, that they may renew their desire and resolution of doing better. The ancient Religious chose for this end the day of their profession and entrance into religion. But as the Daughters of the Visitation should not be attached even to special anniversaries, they have most appropriately selected the festival of the Presentation to make the renewal of their vows with Mary, who offered herself to God on this day. In this action we verify the words of the Prophet David that many virgins would be brought to God after the example of the most blessed Virgin, to be offered to the divine majesty. To do this with more humility, it is very proper that we prepare for it by a retreat of several days, in which to renew our vows, refresh our soul, and strengthen our resolutions. As a skilful player on the lute is accustomed from time to time to tighten or relax its strings in order to tune them to a certain pitch and render them harmonious, so every year, in our retreats, we should test the affections of our soul as to whether they are in accord to intone the canticle of the glory of God and of our own perfection. For this end we make our annual confession, by which we recognize all discordant chords, all immortified affections, all resolutions not faithfully practised; and having thus tightened the pegs of our spiritual lute, we begin again to sing the canticle of divine love, which consists in strict observance. In imitation of our glorious Mistress and under her protection, we offer ourselves on the altar of divine Goodness, to be wholly consumed in the fire of His burning love.

To these animating words of our blessed Founder we have thought it advisable to join an admonition of a worthy servant of God who, speaking of the profit we should draw from solitude, says: "Great talkers ordinarily leave their retreat lovers of silence and retirement; the slothful and lax become fervent, diligent, and prompt to their duty; they who thought only of their own ease are henceforth enemies of corrupt nature and friends of mortification, without which the spiritual life cannot exist. If you have made a good retreat, you should have learned therein to converse meritoriously with God in reverence, humility, union, love, and continual recollection of His divine presence; to converse advantageously with yourself in purity of heart, in solitude, in peace, and in sincere love of your spiritual welfare and hatred of self; to converse well with the Sisters in charity, mutual support, and edification; and, when requisite, to treat with strangers in modesty and devotion, showing them that you live but for God; in short, to converse well with your guardian angel and the saints, by often visiting and remembering them.

May God bestow upon you this grace! *Amen.*

First Convent of the Visitation of Holy Mary, ANNECY, August 15, 1637, commenced under the auspices of the glorious Mother of God.

God be praised!

Contents.

	PAGE
Mother de Chantal to the Sisters of the Visitation.	3
Preface	5
I. Meditation on the Creation	15
II. Meditation on the End for which we were Created	19
III. Meditation on the Benefits of God	23
IV. Meditation on Sin	28
V. Meditation on Death	33
VI. Meditation on Judgment	38
VII. Meditation on Hell	44
VIII. Meditation on Heaven	49
IX. Meditation on Religious Poverty	54
X. Meditation on Obedience	59
XI. Meditation on Chastity	64
XII. Meditation to Assist us to Know our Misery and Weakness	68
XIII. Meditation on the Submission that Our Saviour practised in His Divine Infancy	72

CONTENTS.

		PAGE
XIV.	Meditation on the Incomparable Grace that we possess in being Daughters of Holy Church....................	77
XV.	Meditation on the Particular Benefit of the Religious Vocation..........	82
XVI.	Meditation on the Obligation imposed by the Religious Life of strictly imitating Our Saviour................	87
XVII.	Meditation on the Principal Lessons that Our Saviour teaches the Religious Soul.........................	92
XVIII.	Meditation on the Means by which the Religious Soul ravishes the Heart of her Beloved.....................	97
XIX.	Meditation on the Love of our Neighbor	102
XX.	Meditation on the Garden of Olives...	107
XXI.	Meditation on the Love of Our Saviour in the Midst of His Labors.........	112
XXII.	Meditation on Our Saviour on the Cross............................	116
XXIII.	Meditation on the First five Words that Our Saviour spoke on the Cross.....	121
XXIV.	Meditation on the Blessed Virgin standing at the Foot of the Cross........	126
XXV.	Meditation on the Death of Our Saviour on the Cross..................	131

CONTENTS.

	PAGE
XXVI. Meditation on the Joy and Happiness that the Devout Soul experiences in the Cross	136
XXVII. Meditation on the Resurrection of Our Lord	141
XXVIII. Meditation on the Ascension of Our Lord	146
XXIX. Meditation on the Descent of the Holy Ghost	151
XXX. Meditation on the Presence of God	156
XXXI. Meditation on the Providence of God	160
XXXII. Meditation on the Will of God	165
XXXIII. Meditation on Detachment and on the Conclusion of the Retreat	170
Letter of Mother de Chantal on Retreats	174
Examen for Annual Confessions	179

Meditations for Retreats.

FIRST MEDITATION.

THE CREATION.

I. Point.

WHENCE have we come? The country we have left is nothingness. Where were you, my dear soul, so many years ago? You were nothing. O nothing, without subsistence or being! O nothing, you are my country, in which I long remained unknown, vile, and eternally abject. "I have said," exclaims Job to corruption, "you are my father;" but I have said to nothingness, you are my country. I have been drawn from your dark abyss and from your loathsome cavern.

II. Point.

Who has drawn us from nothingness? Who has given us being? Who is Our Father? As trees in winter hide away their flowers and fruits until they shoot forth and are seen in the proper season, so God willed from all eternity to create you, O my soul! He kept you enclosed in His mind, as it were, in order to produce you when the time should arrive. Ah! are you not happy to be the child of so good a Father?

III. Point.

When I was nothing, and engulfed in nothingness, the will of God decreed to bestow upon me a being at a certain time and in a certain place, as has been done. Our nature, the old Adam, with its evil inclinations, proceeds from nothingness and always tends to its origin, that is, to nothing-

THE CREATION.

ness and sin. From God proceeds our new Adam, our spiritual inclinations, which tend at all times to their origin, that is, to good, to virtue, and to the enjoyment of God.

Affections.

Of myself, then, what am I, if not a true nothing, a child of nothingness? Wretched and miserable, what have I to glory in? Why should I consider myself of any consequence? O nothing! I shall always remember you, and never exalt myself. I shall endeavor to humble my soul, by keeping before its eyes its obscure and wretched origin. Alas! it has nothing in which to glory, yet it would make a display of itself.

O God! what do I not owe to Thy will which, for so many ages, thought of me in the bosom of Thy providence? O holy will! I belong to thee. Make of me, in me, and by me all that may be pleasing to thee, for I am thy work. What an outrage to be rebellious to the will that has produced me and that alone preserves me!

Ah, the human heart! Although surrounded by the vile things of nature, yet at the first glance that it casts upon God, its natural inclination causes it to recognize its centre. Come, then, my poor heart, rise like a spark from the ashes of your lowliness, and render the love and obedience due to your Creator.

SECOND MEDITATION.

THE END FOR WHICH WE WERE CREATED.

I. Point.

REFLECT that God has made us to His image and likeness, in order that we may love Him. It is so true that our heart is created to love its God that, as soon as it dwells attentively on the divinity, it experiences a certain sweet emotion which testifies that God is the God of our heart.

II. Point.

Reflect that, if God had not created man, He would, indeed, have been sovereignly good, but He would not have been actually merciful, in so far as mercy is exercised only toward the miserable. O sweet consolation! The sun was created to enlighten me, the fire to warm me, and so on with other creatures; but you, O my soul, poor and wretched, you were created that you might become the object of the divine mercy.

III. Point.

Reflect, moreover, that you were created to aspire continually to God. Rivers flow unceasingly and, as the Wise Man says, return to the place whence they came. "O God," exclaims St. Augustine, "Thou hast made my heart for Thyself, and it will never find rest but in Thee; yes, Lord, for Thou art the God of my heart, my portion and my inheritance."

Affections.

Return thanks, O my soul, to this divine Master and Author of nature, who daily bestows upon you all the assistance necessary to attain the end for which He created you, which is to love Him. Ah! I was not made for this world. There is a sovereign Artisan who made me for Himself; therefore, I should aspire after and return to Him in order to unite myself to His goodness to which I belong.

O sweet and desirable meeting of the wealth of my God and of my poverty! Ah! how happy I am to be placed in the world for an end so excellent as to proclaim the excess of sovereign goodness!

O all you who are upon the earth, you are pilgrims, created to exclaim with St. Augustine: "O to desire, O to love, O to approach, O to attain to God!" Come, let us go to our lasting city, to the place of our repose. Our hearts should be like the children of Jonadab, who dared not build houses on this earth. O religious soul! prepare yourself well, for the earth upon which you tread is holy, and the place to which you journey is sanctified.

THIRD MEDITATION.

THE BENEFITS OF GOD.

I. Point.

REFLECT that God created us to be, as it were, the perfection and epitome of the universe. He made our soul a treasury of His riches, which caused Daniel to exclaim: "The most high God hath wrought signs and wonders toward me."

II. Point.

Reflect that God has been so liberal toward you, that He has made the whole world for you. Behold, O my soul, the heavens, the earth, and all created things! All things were made for you, some for your use, others for your comfort and pleasure. But how should all be used? As Our

Lord and the saints used them, that is, moderately, holily, and devoutly. How have I made use of them? Extravagantly and in a worldly manner. I have referred them all to myself, I have considered only the pleasure they brought me, like a bad agent to whom much has been confided, but who has misused everything.

III. Point.

Behold, O my soul, the multitude of the benefits which God has imparted to you! You were cared for at your birth, you were baptized, brought up in the Church, withdrawn from the profane crowd, instructed in spiritual things, favored with a thousand lights, urged to a thousand good resolutions. What thanks should you not return for all this! But oh, how unfaithful have you been in this respect! Alas! like a prodigal child, you have abused the blessings and kindness of your Father. Have recourse at all times to Him, for He is goodness itself, and He will receive you.

Affections.

O Lord, how liberally Thou hast enriched this beautiful soul of mine with marvellous gifts! Ah! what happiness it is to have faith in Our Saviour, to hope in Him, to love Him with the desire of yielding implicit obedience to His divine commands! O sovereign Donor, to crown Thy benefits, grant my soul yet more, namely, that it may never abuse Thy divine gifts. Strengthen my faith, confirm my hope, increase my good desires, inflame my affections, that I may become worthy of the supereminent grace of receiving Thy most holy body.

Ah! how can I be ungrateful to so benign and liberal a Saviour, since I know that He has created for me not only all that I behold, all that I taste, and all that I feel, but that His liberality exceeds even this! Eye has not seen, ear has not heard, the great blessings He has in reserve for me, if I prove a loyal servant. O my King, at every moment I experience the effects of Thy liberality, yet seldom do I say to Thee in return, "I thank Thee." As there is not a moment in which I do not enjoy Thy benefits, so not one should go by without my returning heartfelt thanks. O my soul, how shall we do this, except by using the world well and religiously as if we were using it not, so that our whole life may become an act of thanksgiving. To this end we must attach ourselves to the Giver and not to His gifts.

Ah, my Benefactor! if David exclaimed, "What shall I render to the Lord for all the things that He hath rendered to me?" should not the Christian, should not the religious soul be in still greater perplexity to find a worthy return for Thy favors? O God of all goodness, if I offer myself as a holocaust, it is still very little. Thou askest me for my heart. Take it, O Lord. I give it to Thee. May it never again return to my possession.

FOURTH MEDITATION.

SIN.

I. Point.

We do not fear sin, because we do not sufficiently reflect upon its evil, for sin is called a turning away from God and a turning to the creature; and it is in this withdrawal from God that the principal malice of sin consists. Alas! how often you have withdrawn from this good God! Ah! my soul, is it possible that you could take pleasure in turning away from the Source of all good, in order to follow the path of sin?

II. Point.

Reflect that there are many unfortunate steps by which the soul descends to perdition: ingratitude; attention to worldly affairs, which withdraw the mind from heavenly things; the habit of yielding to frivolous and superfluous thoughts; and a certain detestable custom of speaking ill of our neighbor. By remarking the faults of others, we lose shame for our own transgressions; we neglect to have recourse to God by prayer; and finally, we precipitate ourselves so deeply into sin that we coolly drink in iniquity like water. O soul, destined for eternal delights! I picture to you this unfortunate descent, that you may withdraw your feet from evil ways.

III. Point.

Reflect that, like Cain, they are lost who do not aim at making a good confession, or who make it through routine without true sorrow for their sins and a firm purpose of amendment. They, on the contrary, are saved with the good thief and with Job who do not conceal their sins, but who sincerely accuse themselves of them. Ah! we sin in innumerable ways, by omission, commission, and inadvertence. Religious, removed from occasions of grievous sin, deceive themselves if they esteem their faults slight, and neglect to have compunction for them. No matter how small the sin may be, it is a base ingratitude toward God, who knows fully the gravity of our faults, though we may not be aware of it.

Affections.

Come, my soul, let us draw near to God, for He receives sinners. Let us not leave our Jesus. It is He who calls us. "Return, return," says He, "erring children who forsake your Father." O Lord! behold I come to Thee, because Thou hast called me. Receive me according to Thy

SIN.

word, and I shall live. No never, Lord, with the help of Thy grace, never will I withdraw from Thee. Alas! I have sinned too frequently, but I now repent with all my heart.

O God of clemency, Thy mercy is greater than my iniquity! If Thou wouldst reprove me according to Thy justice, what would become of me? I see that there is not one wicked step upon which I have not placed my foot. O my Father! I have sinned against heaven and before Thee. Though I am not worthy to be called Thy child, I still aspire to that happiness.

O Lord! assisted by Thy holy grace, I will in future sorrowfully accuse myself of my sins. I will never again consider any fault trifling, since so great a God is offended by it. Ah, Lord! Thou art patient and Thou dost defer the punishment of the sinner; but Thou wilt not remain silent, if he does not amend. Hence, O my wretched heart, annihilate yourself in contrition and penance, by the consideration of the infinite goodness of God whom you have offended, and determine rather to die than to sin voluntarily. O Lord! Thou seest the weakness of my heart. Strengthen me, that my resolution may become efficacious.

FIFTH MEDITATION.

DEATH.

I. Point.

REFLECT, O mortals, that it would be a great offence against God to die without having thought of death. Death, which dominates over this perishable life, observes no fixed rules; at one time it takes this person, at another that, without choice or method, the good and the bad, the young and the old. O how blessed are they who live in a continual fear of death, and who are at all times prepared so to die, that they may live forever in that life in which there is no death!

II. Point.

Reflect that God, having placed us in the house of this world, will, on a day known to Himself and of which we are ignorant, call us before Him with this summons: "Give an account of thy stewardship, of thy vows, of thy Rules, and observances; in short, of all the possessions over which I have placed thee." Alas! what will be the outcome of this reckoning? I do not know; for all this is hidden in the future.

III. Point.

Reflect that the just man does not die an unprovided death, for he has amply provided for the dread moment by persevering in Christian integrity and in religious obedience. Moreover, holy Church does not pray that we may not die a sudden, but an unprovided, death.

Affections.

If the religious state secured us no other boon than that of a constant preparation

DEATH.

for death, we ought to hold it in great respect. Alas! my soul, death teaches us every day that the glory of this world is naught but illusion and falsehood, and that the life of man passes away as a puff of wind. Come, then, let us cast ourselves at the feet of our immortal King, to whom death is more amiable than the life of all the kings of the earth. O sweet Jesus! bestow upon me that lasting remembrance of death which destroys sin, which humiliates me by causing me to think of the dust of the tomb, and which makes me despise all that is perishable.

O blessed Father, St. Francis, you did not die an unprovided death, you who meditated so profoundly on death, who were so well prepared to hear the final summons, and who said: "I am about to prepare myself, to put myself in readiness for the great journey to eternity." Ah!

that I may be faithful to the practice which you have ordained for us, to regret the hours passed unprofitably, since we must render an account of all on the day of our death. Take care, O my dear soul, how you observe every rule and vow of your Institute; for I warn you that you must render an account of all to our sovereign Judge. O Jesus, remember that Thou art at the same time my Judge and my Father, my Saviour and my Examiner!

"Alas! when I think how ill I have employed the time of God, I am in doubt whether or not He will give me share in His eternal happiness, since He gives it only to those who employ well this present time," exclaimed the holy Founder. If this faithful servant said this of himself, what should I, sinful spendthrift, say of myself? O my sweet Jesus, covered with confusion before Thee, I beseech Thee to enter not into an exact account with Thy servant; for who can withstand Thy anger? Rather grant me this grace that, in imitation of my blessed Father, I may be so anxious to serve Thee well, that I may confidently abandon to Thee the entire care of my death.

SIXTH MEDITATION.

JUDGMENT.

I. Point.

REFLECT, O my soul, that you are truly senseless if you tremble not at the remembrance of the Last Day, when consuming fire will go before the Judge, when thunder and whirlwinds will roar around Him, when the waters will rise and cast out fiery flames, and the monsters of the deep and the beasts of the earth will howl most frightfully. When the Judge shall appear, the heavens will be shaken, the stars will fall at His feet, the moon will become like blood, and the sun will be obscured. O God, what a convulsion of nature! But it is God alone who does this, for the universe is so noble that no one can destroy it save its Creator.

II. Point.

Reflect that God, being on the judgment seat, with all the nations of the world before Him, will, like a shepherd, separate the goats from the sheep. He will, in an admirable manner, imprint on the minds of the reprobate dread of the loss which they are about to sustain. The divine Majesty will show them clearly the beauty of His face, and the treasures of His goodness. At the sight of that infinite abyss of delight, their will, by a supreme effort, will seek to rush toward God, in order to unite itself to Him and to enjoy His love, but that will be impossible. From the instant that the divine beauty penetrates the understanding of these unfortunate beings, the divine justice will so deprive their will of strength that it will be unable to love that most amiable Object. They will hear this frightful sentence: "Depart from Me, you cursed, into everlasting fire!"

III. Point.

And the Judge turning to His dear sheep: "Come," He will say, "ye blessed of My Father, possess the kingdom prepared for you." Then the commandment to love shall give way to the command of happiness, and we shall see that the commandment of love, which the King Jesus gave to the citizens of Jerusalem militant, was given only that they might merit citizenship in Jerusalem triumphant.

Affections.

O sovereign Judge, when Thou shalt have enclosed all humanity in eternity, Thou shalt break the shell of this visible

JUDGMENT. 41

world. I adore Thy power, but I invoke Thy mercy. For if on that day of Thy wrath the pillars of heaven are shaken, how greatly shall my poor heart be disturbed which, like a straw, is agitated by every wind? Alas, O good God! Thou wilt render to every one according to his works; therefore, I should strive only to do well, for that will be the day of Thy general reward. Yes, even the earth, O my God, which has supported Thy elect, will be changed in form, and made more transparent than a mirror; the sun will have seven times more light than it now possesses, and the moon will be made bright as the sun. Oh, what happiness to behold the King, Jesus on the day of His triumph!

What do I say! On that day, alas! what advantage will it be to the wicked to see God, if they cannot love Him? Lord! deliver me from that eternal misfortune and from the never-ending despair of those that will find themselves not only unable to love Thy goodness, but will even feel an aversion for it.

My soul, now is the time to judge, to condemn, to correct yourself, and to acquire the solid virtues of your vocation; for even if on that fearful day, you should be able to say: "Lord, I have raised the dead, I have wrought miracles in Thy name," you will not fail to hear these terrible words: "Go, worker of iniquity, I know you not, for you have not observed your vows and Rules."

O holy and happy company, may you be eternally blessed! Ah! you are indeed blessed, because you have been docile and obedient as sheep. Grant, O sweet Jesus, my kind Master, that I may bless Thee during the course of this life by good works, so that Thou wilt bless me throughout eternity, and give a place at Thy right to the work of Thy hands.

HELL.

SEVENTH MEDITATION.

HELL.

I. Point.

REFLECT that, after the judgment, the condemned souls will be united to their bodies, the accomplices of their guilt and the companions of their punishment, and will enter into their loathsome abode, to dwell eternally in that place of darkness, in which horror and fearful confusion reign.

II. Point.

The unfortunate beings will remain in their infernal prison, filled with despairing rage at the remembrance of that unparalleled happiness which they will never possess, because, when they could have

HELL. 45

loved and served God, they refused to do so. This teaches me that I should work whilst I have the light.

III. Point.

Reflect that, above all their other torments, they will burn with a thirst made the more violent by the remembrance of the eternal fountains. They will forever be like mad dogs, perishing with hunger, rendered all the more gnawing by the recollection of the eternal banquet of which they are deprived. Cursing one another, they will unite in blaspheming their Creator, for they know that for all eternity they will be utterly wretched.

Affections.

O God, when I behold Adam and Eve departing from the terrestrial paradise (after having been loaded with so many graces), crushed by the weight of their sins and full of misery, I am forced to exclaim: Who are they that are quitting paradise overwhelmed with woe? I am astounded. But, O Saviour of the world, I am still more astonished when I see a soul nourished in the paradise of the Church, enriched with her treasures, susceptible of eternal happiness, descending through her own fault into eternal perdition. "Alas, O God, my God!" I say, "She could have been Thy spouse, and behold she is Thy enemy! She could have enjoyed Thy Church triumphant, and behold, she is a citizen of the infernal Babylon!" O sin! O self-will! It is you that have led this unfortunate creature into this disaster, and, consequently, it is you whom I detest with all my might.

Hasten, O religious souls, to serve God, to enter into the narrow way of all our

HELL.

observances, for it conducts to life. O my sweet Jesus! turn away my feet from that broad and deceitful route, a route sensual, wilful, and worldly, which conducts to eternal death, and upon which so many enter. Preserve me from following the broad and tortuous path which leads hypocrites to perdition.

"O religious souls! you have so many means to perfect yourselves, you are on the mystical ladder which reaches to heaven. Alas! if, through your own unworthiness, you cast yourselves into the eternal abyss, if you are profoundly buried therein, it will be in the lowest depths," says a holy contemplative. O most blessed Virgin, never permit that any one of the sheep of your flock be rejected with the infernal goats and wolves.

O Mother of all sweetness, I fly from hell, because there you and your Son are not loved. The blessed would consider themselves damned, if they were for a moment deprived of this love. O Mother of fair love, grant that I may begin so to love, as for all eternity to love your divine Son!

EIGHTH MEDITATION.

HEAVEN.

I. Point.

REFLECT that God, who is more inclined to reward than to punish, will bestow infinite glory upon His elect; He will place them in His triumphant kingdom. O how delightful is this abode! It is a paradise of beauty, splendor, and happiness. " O city of God, holy Jerusalem," says St. Augustine, " how transported will my soul be to behold thy glory, thy beauty, thy gates, thy walls, thy streets! Thy mansions are of precious stones, thy gates of fine pearls, thy streets of most pure gold; nothing enters into thee which is not most perfect. In short, O holy Jerusalem, thou art truly beautiful, and sweet in thy delights."

II. Point.

Reflect how good it is to see this city, in which the great King is seated on His throne, surrounded by His blessed servants. There we behold the choirs of angels singing hymns, and the full assembly of the celestial citizens; there are the venerable troop of prophets, the full number of the apostles, the victorious army of innumerable martyrs, the august rank of pontiffs, the sacred body of confessors, the true and perfect religious, holy women, humble widows, pure virgins. Their glory is not equal; but their bliss is the same, for in heaven reigns full and perfect charity.

III. Point.

Reflect that for all eternity these blessed souls will enjoy supreme happiness; that

HEAVEN. 51

God gives Himself to them in His entirety; and that the eternal Son says benignly to His Father: "Father, I wish that they whom Thou hast given Me may remain eternally with Me, and that they may behold the light which I received from Thee before the creation of the world." And addressing His dear children: "Have I not told you that whoever would love Me, would be loved by My Father, and that we would manifest ourselves to him?" Then this holy company, inundated with delight in the bosom of the divinity, will chant an eternal *Alleluia* of gratitude and praise to their Creator.

Affections.

I salute you from afar, O my holy mother Jerusalem, filled with all beauty, illuminated by the Sun of justice! The pure and immaculate Lamb is your beautiful and resplendent light, your brightness, and all your beatitude. O God of life, how desirable is Thy palace! That is the place in which Thou diffusest Thy delights. Ah! wretched moment of this mortal life, I cannot love you, except so far as you aid me to arrive at this blessed eternity. Alas! how wearisome to me is the earth, and how displeasing are its pleasures, when I turn my eyes toward you, O my beloved Sion!

Blessed courtiers of this great King, you realize now, in the joy of Our Lord, that he who is faithful in little is placed over many things. Ah, tell me by what path have you arrived at this happy abode? Some by patience, by faith, by hope, by meekness, but all and every one by charity and humility. I am placed here below to ascend the same steps by the practice of the holy virtues. Grant me your assistance, lest my frailty should cause me rather to fall back than to ascend to your much desired and beautiful assembly.

Courage, my soul, let us labor and combat! The blessed kingdom is bestowed only upon conquerors. But, O my God, Thou art my beatitude, therefore I desire Thee alone, Thou God of paradise, and not the paradise of God. Ah, what a favor, to behold forever the Spouse in His glory, the Lord face to face, to love and to bless Him eternally!

NINTH MEDITATION.

RELIGIOUS POVERTY.

I. Point.

BLESSED are the poor in spirit, for theirs is the kingdom of heaven; cursed, therefore, are the rich in spirit, who are attached to the things of this world, for the misery of hell is their portion. You have vowed poverty. O how happy you are if you observe it faithfully, and how honored should you not regard yourself to belong to so blessed a company! Our Lord, Our Lady, St. Joseph, were poor; love, then, this holy virtue as the dear friend of Jesus Christ, who lived and died in poverty.

II. Point.

Reflect that to be poor means to be in

need, to want many things. Behold the example of the poor and divine Jesus: "The foxes," says He, "have their dens in the forest; and the birds of the air, nests; but the Son of man has no place whereon to rest His head." O Religious! who have vowed to be poor with Jesus Christ, do you not blush with shame for wishing at all times to have your desires gratified and to want for nothing? You should desire and rejoice to want even the necessaries of life. You should, I repeat, be delighted, if like your Spouse you have not whereon to rest your head.

III. *Point.*

Weigh seriously the obligation of your vow. You should live not only in perfect abnegation of the things that you use, but still more in poverty, entirely despoiled of all things, according to your Constitutions.

By which you should remember that a Religious injures herself, and is not poor, who is attached to time, to places, to creatures, to esteem, to consolations. All these things constitute her riches; and, as a matter of fact, she is not possessed of that nudity of heart and poverty of spirit of which she makes profession.

Affections.

I return thanks to Thee, O Lord, since Thy goodness has placed me in this abode where, among Thy spouses, the words *thine* and *mine* are not heard except on this one occasion, in which the loving soul is permitted to exclaim: "My Beloved is all mine!" Ah, Lord! give me a true love for this much esteemed poverty with all its wants and inconveniences. Defend me from the ambition that too frequently desires the honor of being considered poor, while at the same time enjoying all the conveniences of wealth.

O my God! I should humble myself profoundly at seeing Thee, the King of all things, having not even a place whereon to rest Thy head, and myself, miserable worm of the earth, so well provided with all necessaries. My ingratitude attains to this degree, that in a convent, the holy house of the poor, I look for superfluities and all the conveniences appertaining to worldlings, although, perhaps, I did not enjoy them when in the world. O Lord! who embraced poverty for love of me, I throw myself at Thy feet in order to repent of this disorder.

Yes, O Lord, I wish to observe my vow with great fidelity. I shall cherish and conceal between Thee and myself the small privations that may befall me. I shall love vile and coarse things, as truly appertaining to me. In short, I beg of Thee this grace, that during the remainder of my life I may be poor in my employments, at work, in food, in clothing, in sickness, in health, and in everything.

God of all goodness, who said in ancient times: "I do not wish that they who serve in My temple should possess an inheritance; for I desire to be their portion." O my Lord! why is it that so many Religious do not possess Thee, if not because they wish to possess something else? Come, then, my soul, let us strip ourselves of everything. Depart from me, possessions and conveniences of the body; begone, vain consolations; depart, superfluous affections; henceforth I desire to live in total privation of all things. I wish to render my vows to God, who is my portion, my heritage, my eternal possession, and whom I shall enjoy the less the more I enjoy anything but Him.

TENTH MEDITATION.

OBEDIENCE.

I. Point.

REFLECT that you have vowed religious obedience. It is an entire surrender (says St. Climacus) of all human desires; a voluntary death, a life without curiosity, an assured road which seeks no excuse before God, a secure voyage, a tomb of self-will, and a giving life to humility. Ah, how badly you have practised a virtue so exalted! If you do not observe it as you should, you will expose your soul to all the sins opposed to the above-mentioned virtue.

II. Point.

In order to animate yourself still further to the practice of this holy virtue, consider our sweet Jesus in the house of St. Joseph, retired from the world, and obedient in all things. There it was that He originated the monastic life. But, my God, in what does He obey? In things low and vile, in helping to draw a saw, or handle a plane, He, the God of majesty and glory! And we, poor insignificant creatures, abject beyond expression, hesitate to obey if some glory and satisfaction are not connected with our act of obedience.

III. Point.

Revolve in your mind these blessed words of Our Saviour: "I am not come into the world to do My own will, but that of My Father who sent Me;" and say: "O my God, I have not entered the convent to do my will, but that of my celestial Father, who sent me hither by His inspirations, which I behold in my Rules, in my

OBEDIENCE.

observances, and in all that my Superiors ordain for me." Assuredly, the Religious who wishes to do her own will in the convent does not imitate her divine Spouse; therefore, on the Day of Judgment she will deserve to be judged with worldlings and the refractory. O God, what confusion!

Affections.

Lord, I admit that in obedience all is safe, and that out of it all is precarious. Alas! I have acted very wrongfully in allowing my self-will to live! I have renounced my vows and my profession. Ah, what a misfortune! I have resumed the care of self, after having abandoned myself entirely to Thee. O Lord! I repent of my fault. Henceforth, casting myself into the arms of obedience and of my Superiors, I resolve, with the assistance of Thy grace, to walk blindly, regarding not where they lead me, but only the assured path in which I walk, namely, to Thy blessed eternity.

O my sweet and obedient Saviour! how deluded I have been to prefer obedience in great to obedience in small matters! No, my God, do not permit this misfortune to befall me, but cause me to regard with the eyes of faith lowly things as exercises in which I can more easily imitate Thy holy humanity, abased and humiliated. Never permit me, therefore, to murmur at anything that may be commanded, nor to criticise the employments that may be given me; but, with sincere affection, may I consider that my food and my sweetest nourishment is in all things to practise holy obedience!

O self-judgment, betrayer of my will, it is time for me to crush you, else you will

OBEDIENCE.

annihilate me. Ah, my God! I do not wish to restrain my own will because at all times it leads me into evil, but because it prevents me from following Thee. O Thou who wert obedient unto death, even unto the death of the cross, grant that I may live and die only by obedience! Our Saviour did not desire to do His own most blessed will. Shall I ever, then, dare to do my will, which is altogether corrupt?

ELEVENTH MEDITATION.

CHASTITY.

I. Point.

CONSIDER the favor that God has done you in choosing you for His spouse, since a woman ordinarily changes her condition for that of her husband, and becomes a queen if he is a king. Reflect with what reverence you should esteem this grace. "They have become abominable as the things that they have loved," says the Prophet, speaking of the wicked. And we can say of the good, that they become as amiable as the things that they love.

II. Point.

Behold to what happiness God has called you! They who live in the world run great

CHASTITY.

risk of offering to God a divided heart and, consequently, of hearing the heavenly Spouse refuse it, saying: "No one can serve two masters." But souls that have absolutely left all in order to consecrate themselves to God, are delivered from that danger. They should secure the door of their heart with the bar of a chaste fear, that nothing may enter therein but what relates to the love and service of their Spouse.

III. Point.

Revolve in your mind the interior perfection to which this vow obliges you. Reflect upon the words of your Rule, which gives you no other liberty than that of living, sighing, and breathing but for your celestial Spouse. If you are obliged to hold converse with others, let it be immaculate and angelic. Ah, how blessed are the pure of heart, for they shall see God!

Affections.

O Jesus, dear Spouse of pure souls! I admire the excess of Thy goodness which, having made choice of me for a dignity so great as to be Thy spouse, has not rejected me, although I have so frequently been wanting in fidelity. I return a thousand thanks to Thy sovereign sweetness. My soul, humble yourself profoundly before the great army of virgins who follow the Lamb and His blessed Mother whithersoever they go. Supplicate them to offer you to Jesus, the King of virgins. Let us be devout to our good angel, for these celestial spirits take pleasure in guarding the bed of King Solomon, namely, the soul that is pure, humble, devout, and faithful.

My Beloved, in order to keep the garden of my heart for Thee alone, grant me the grace to surround it with the thorns of

CHASTITY.

holy mortification and to close the doors and windows of my senses, so that not one of my thoughts may stray out. Grant, also, that my entire soul may remain exclusively occupied with Thee, O my only Consolation, my most sweet Retreat!

When shall it be, O my God, that, assisted by Thy grace, I shall walk in my way according to the full extent of my obligations, and that the words of my vows shall be always before my eyes, so that, avoiding distractions, immortification of the senses, useless preoccupation of mind, I may aspire after and breathe but for Thee? Grant me this grace, O my most dear God! May the things of this world turn into bitterness and mortification for me, that Thou alone mayst be balm to my soul, and that my thoughts may find pleasure but in Thy sovereign sweetness!

TWELFTH MEDITATION.

TO ASSIST US TO KNOW OUR MISERY AND WEAKNESS.

I. Point.

WHAT is a human being but miserable smoke which is soon dissipated, or, as Job says, " a leaf of a tree agitated by the wind, the sport of evils, inconstancy without firmness, and in the end the prey of the tomb"? Still more, this misery has attained to such a degree by the liberty of his depraved will, that it converts almost everything into his own wretchedness, and, finally, breaks his neck on the sharp stone placed for his support and protection.

II. Point.

Reflect that, being so impotent, what can

OUR MISERY AND WEAKNESS. 69

you do of yourself? Ah! you can do much evil and no good. You can fall into a thousand sins, and remain in this lamentable condition without being able to arise from it of yourself, until Our Lord, by sending light, fears, remorse, and salutary warnings, makes you return to Him. Exclaim, then, with St. Augustine: "O Lord, without Thee I can die, but without Thee never shall I be able to find the road to life."

III. Point.

Reflect, moreover, that your frailty is so intense that, being on the road of virtue, you could not walk of yourself, if Our Lord did not continually watch over you. You would disgrace yourself at every moment, and in the end you would go astray.

O religious souls, beware that Our Lord does not address this reproach to you: "Israel was weak, and I conducted her

Myself; but she escaped from My hand, and she is lost."

Affections.

O Lord, come to my aid! Make haste to help me! Alas! I am but an atom, a nothing, and I desire to elevate myself.

O my God, I exclaim with David, Thou art my Father, my God, and the rock of my salvation! Deliver me from the guidance of my self-will, and let Thy right hand support Thy foolish servant.

But, O my God, if in my misery I should chance to fall into the dreadful precipice of sin, do Thou regard me with a favorable eye! Without Thy assistance, I cannot even form the thought of leaving that abyss. My dear soul, understand your misery and, in consequence of it, remain profoundly humble and dependent upon your divine Spouse.

OUR MISERY AND WEAKNESS. 71

Lord, I acknowledge that my beginning, my perseverance, and my end depend upon Thee. Ah, if Thy goodness had not long assisted me in the past, I should have perished! O Leader of Israel, never, with the aid of Thy grace, will I leave Thy sweet hand, which guides and conducts me by the way of Thy holy will. Ah! rather, Lord, let Thy right hand be placed under my head, and Thy left hand embrace me! Then I shall see that I have nothing but what I have received from Thy bounty. In what can I glory except in being nothing, and in proclaiming that my God is all things to me?

THIRTEENTH MEDITATION.

THE SUBMISSION THAT OUR SAVIOUR PRACTISED IN HIS DIVINE INFANCY.

I. Point.

CONSIDER, in the first place, the submission of the eternal Son to the will of His heavenly Father, knowing that He wished to save mankind. He offered Himself, He condescended to come upon earth, and to conceal Himself in the chaste womb of the most blessed Virgin. He who was greatness itself, omnipotent, omniscient, all-perfect, did not refuse, or as the Church sings, He had no horror of that narrow and obscure prison, because such was the will of His Father.

II. Point.

Reflect that our good Saviour, having submitted to the office of Redeemer of men, submitted absolutely to all that depended thereon. He was satisfied to hide His eternal wisdom under the veil of infancy; and He, the uncreated Word, condescended to keep silence until He had attained the age at which other children speak. In short, that rich, strong, immortal One condescended to appear as poor and as weak as His own creatures; and I, a wretched worm of the earth, I wish to show myself, I wish to speak, I wish to exalt myself!

III. Point.

Reflect to what a degree the submission of our divine Saviour extended, since the Evangelist says that He was obedient to the Blessed Virgin and to the glorious St. Joseph. He abandoned Himself entirely to their guidance, to be taken up, to be carried, to be put down, with total indifference, for the reason, doubtless, that He regarded them as persons commissioned by His eternal Father to protect Him in His sacred infancy.

Affections.

O eternal God, Father of Our Lord Jesus Christ, who for our good sent Thy Son down from heaven to assume our life, in order that He might bestow upon us His own life, fill my heart with affections of gratitude, and my lips with acts of thanksgiving in return for this benefit. O sweet Jesus! if, according to my unworthiness, I might imitate Thy submission, how happy I should be! When obedience sends me here or leaves me there, or destines me for any occupation, I should find no place too humble, too inconvenient; all should be acceptable to my will, if it was submis-

OUR SAVIOUR'S SUBMISSION.

sive to that of my heavenly Father. Is it possible, O my God! that I behold Thee undertake so much for me, and that I am willing to undertake nothing for Thee? You must, my dear soul, be courageous, in order to imitate your Spouse, and ascend to Him by this happy descent of submission and resignation of self.

O my Lord! since in obedience to Thee I have followed my religious vocation, I now wish in imitation of Thee and assisted by Thy grace and Thy example, to submit myself to all that depends upon and appertains to my state of life. Being nothing, I desire to appear as nothing; having become a little child in order to gain the kingdom of heaven, I shall remain in silence, not knowing, as it were, how to speak except through charity or necessity. Behold the desires of my heart! But, O sweet and divine Infant! I expect from Thee and not from myself the grace, the strength, and the fidelity of which I have need to accomplish my purpose.

What dost Thou teach me, O my divine Master, by Thy submission to the blessed Virgin and to St. Joseph, except to ask for nothing and to refuse nothing, and to remain wholly dependent on the will and direction of the Superiors that my heavenly Father has placed over me? Ah, my God, how ashamed I should be to see Thee obedient in all things, and myself so frequently rebellious! Permit no longer, O Lord, this misfortune to befall me, but grant me the favor that, while adoring Thy submission, I may begin the practice of the same holy virtue.

FOURTEENTH MEDITATION.

THE INCOMPARABLE GRACE THAT WE POSSESS IN BEING DAUGHTERS OF HOLY CHURCH.

I. Point.

CONSIDER that Jesus Christ came into this world to establish His holy Church, the Mother of all the children of salvation. It is a work so excellent that He constituted Himself its architect. "Blessed art thou," said He, "thou art Peter, and on this rock I will build My Church, and the gates of hell shall not prevail against it."

II. Point.

Behold the majesty and sanctity of this Church. Jesus is her Head, and she is His matchless spouse. Whoever is not a child of this holy Mother cannot be a child of God. O how rich she is! The keys of heaven are bestowed upon her, the sacraments are her treasures, and Jerusalem triumphant is her sister.

III. Point.

Consider the incomparable grace that God has granted you in making you daughters of this Church. This reflection formed all the glory of the saints. "I value nothing," said St. Catharine, "except to be a Christian." And a martyr sang when dying: "I am the son of a Mother, the most holy Church, whose true children can never die." St. Teresa could not sufficiently thank God for being a daughter of His Church.

St. Francis de Sales made his happiness in this world consist in laboring, and even sacrificing his life, for the service of this true spouse of Jesus Christ. "Ah!" he

THE INCOMPARABLE GRACE. 79

exclaimed, "how incomparably animated do I feel my courage to serve more faithfully than ever the Church of the living God, and the living God of the Church." In short, all the saints had no other delight. They were consumed with gratitude; and you very probably have never thought of returning thanks to God for so signal a benefit.

Affections.

Were my heart to melt with love and thanksgiving toward Thee, O Lord, for having built this Church for us, I would not yet have fulfilled my obligation. When I reflect upon the thought, I cannot refrain from exclaiming with David: "Blessed be the work of the hands of my God; and may He be ever blessed in His work."

I salute you, incomparable dove without stain, pillar of strength, house of the King!

Mother most benign, who dost receive repentant sinners and reconcile them to God! Mother most sweet, who dost feed her children with the bread of life and make them drink even of the blood of the Spouse! Ah, why should I not love my religious vocation! Assuredly, O my God, I believe that Thou hast given it to me, that I may become a most devoted daughter of so glorious a Mother. O holy spouse of the divine Spouse! assisted by your grace, I desire to embrace all your maxims, and to drink of your doctrine as a beverage of salvation.

My soul, be confounded! O Lord, what am I that Thou hast placed me in this tabernacle of the just, among the assembly of Thy glorious apostles, of Thy victorious martyrs, of Thy venerable pontiffs and confessors, of Thy most pure virgins and of all Thy beloved elect! I confess, O my

THE INCOMPARABLE GRACE.

God, that it is the grace of graces, and that Thy predilection alone has imparted it to me. O holy assembly of the elect of my Saviour Jesus, who will obtain for me this favor, except my God, that by your prayers, I may not become unworthy of your society; but that rather in this world, as a generous daughter of the Church, I may never cease to triumph over myself and make progress in virtue, until I reach Jerusalem triumphant in your sweet company.

FIFTEENTH MEDITATION.

THE PARTICULAR BENEFIT OF THE RELIGIOUS VOCATION.

I. Point.

REFLECT that Solomon, having regarded all things that are under the heavens, protests that "all is vanity, and affliction of spirit." What, then, do we leave for God when we enter the religious life? Nothing but phantoms and appearances of good; and if the prophets inform us that all things are as if they did not exist before Thee, if all is but nothing, O my God, what have we left personally? Our misery is always extreme. We are so blind that we persuade ourselves that we have done great things for Thee in abandoning these nothings, while all the time it is Thou, O Lord, who hast done great things for us in leading us to renounce them.

II. Point.

Reflect that you were not capable of choosing a vocation so holy. It is God who, in His incomparable love, has called you to it, constraining you without violence to depart from Sodom and to enter into His banquet. The religious life is not a natural one. It is elevated above nature. It is, therefore, necessary that grace should bestow it and be its soul.

III. Point.

Consider what gratitude you should testify to our divine Lord and Saviour, who has deigned through the instrumentality of His blessed Mother, to change the water of your life into wine; that is, to turn your faults into virtues, and to make you all His. Ask of God great thankfulness for this grace, which is not less than the grace of vocation. The ingratitude of the children of Israel, withdrawn from the bondage of Egypt into the solitude of the desert, so greatly irritated the Lord that He wished to exterminate them one and all.

Affections.

Lord, what have I left in quitting the world, but poverty full of care, or some miserable possession full of inquietude? I have abandoned trouble, anguish, dissension, continual occasions of losing my soul; and Thou hast given me a life sweet, tranquil, full of holy union and furnished with a thousand means of raising my soul to Thee. O my God! I admit that Thou hast done much for me, and that I have done nothing for Thee, by entering upon this vocation. I am a useless servant; moreover,

I am ungrateful, if I do not fulfil the end for which Thou didst call me to Thy blessed service.

What return shall I make to Thee, O my God, for this most precious benefit which Thou hast bestowed upon me? I will fulfil my vows to Thee by a punctual observance before all Thy people; that is to say, O my King, that, assisted by Thy grace, I will live the life of a true Religious, my soul at all times elevated to Thee, doing continual violence to nature, loving self-contempt, never blaming those that blame me, nor leaving the strait and narrow road which conducts to life eternal. O most blessed Virgin! since it is by your intercession that I have received the grace to dwell in your house all the days of my life, help me to live there in such a manner that you will not refuse to acknowledge me as your daughter.

Lord, Thou didst say in times past: " What can I do for Israel that I have not done?" Ah! it seems to me that the following words are addressed to my soul: " O thoughtless Religious, what has Our Lord not done for you? And you do not return the gratitude due Him. Oh! you should delight to find yourself out of Egypt, to keep yourself amorously retired, to fly from everything that appertains to the world; but on the contrary, you irritate your Spouse by seeking more earnestly, perhaps, your satisfactions and conveniences than you did when in the world." O my Beloved, I admit that I have not deserved to taste Thy sweet manna. But for the future I renounce everything; I am dead to the world. A thousand times I bless the day on which I died, in order to live only for Thee.

SIXTEENTH MEDITATION.

THE OBLIGATION IMPOSED BY THE RELIGIOUS LIFE OF STRICTLY IMITATING OUR SAVIOUR.

I. Point.

CONSIDER that Our Saviour when calling His disciples, always said to them: "Follow Me." When they were fishing, like St. Peter and St. Andrew; or mending their nets, like the children of Zebedee; or at the counting-house, like St. Matthew,—all received the same summons: "Follow Me." From this I learn that all who are called to the religious life and to evangelical perfection, are called to imitate the Saviour in His humanity, and to practise virtue after His example.

II. Point.

Reflect in what manner you should follow Our Saviour. Learn it from His own words: "Whoever will come after Me," says He, "let him deny himself and follow Me." But, O divine Saviour! whither shall we follow Thee? Throughout Thy entire life Thou didst tread the road of perfect poverty, of contempt, humiliation and abjection before creatures, and of incessant labor. Is it in this way that we should follow Thee? Is it in these paths that the Religious obliges herself to follow in Thy footprints? O immense, but precious, abnegation!

III. Point.

Consider into what a misfortune they fall who, after having consecrated themselves to Thee, O my Saviour, and having commenced to follow Thee, turn back. "Alas!" says He, "they are no more fit for the kingdom of heaven" than they who

IMITATING OUR SAVIOUR.

practise virtue on some occasions only and hesitate on others. "I say to you weeping," said the fervent St. Paul, "that there are some among you who walk enemies of Jesus Christ, whose end is perdition."

Affections.

O Lord, of whom it is written, that, having ascended the mountain, Thou didst call to Thee those whom Thou didst desire to be Thy disciples! Ah! I come to Thee on the mount of religious perfection, because Thou hast called me. Receive me according to Thy word and I shall live. But, my sweet Saviour, how shall I follow Thee— Thou who, the Prophet assures us, hast come from the highest heavens to run Thy course in this world as a giant? Ah! Thou Thyself must be my strength and my fleetness. O negligent Religious! why do you follow your Spouse at such a distance? Do you not care to approach Him? If you wish to reach Him, follow Him without hesitation; for in following Him, whoever hesitates goes back; whoever does not advance recedes.

O self, I renounce you, as only on this condition can I follow my Jesus. O holy cross of my vocation, I embrace you with my whole soul, since it is with you and by you I must follow my Spouse. Divine Spouse! who trod the paths of a life hidden, afflicted, suffering, and despised, dilate my heart, that I may run after Thee on this blessed road. O religious souls! if you would turn away from all distractions, if you would renounce yourselves absolutely, the fragrance of the Beloved, His sacred example, would draw you, and you would run after the odor of His divine perfumes.

Oh, what a deplorable thing to behold

IMITATING OUR SAVIOUR. 91

so many slothful and lukewarm souls, who hesitate at every moment on the road of perfection! O Divine Master! who hast called me because of Thy love for me, grant by Thy grace that I may follow Thee, not at a distance, but close on Thy steps according to my ability. O religious soul, let the dead bury the dead; but you who have found your Jesus, your life and your way, follow Him!

SEVENTEENTH MEDITATION.

THE PRINCIPAL LESSONS THAT OUR SAVIOUR
TEACHES THE RELIGIOUS SOUL.

I. Point.

CONSIDER that our meek Jesus, having come into the world and established the religious life, gives as His first lesson to His beloved novices: " Learn of Me, for I am meek and humble of Heart, and you shall find rest for your souls." O my soul! cast yourself at the feet of your Spouse. Listen to His divine doctrine of meekness, humility, and peace. Ponder on it in the depth of your heart, and make it the basis of your piety, your perfection, and your salvation.

II. Point.

Passing on to another lesson of perfection, let us hear what Jesus says to all His disciples: "Unless you become as little children, you shall not enter into the kingdom of heaven." O lesson of innocence, of simplicity, of uprightness, of perfect submission! What, O Lord! if we are not like little children, we shall not enter into the kingdom of heaven? Ah! that is a threat. We do not sufficiently weigh its importance.

III. Point.

As the third precept this good Master teaches that we must work, pray without ceasing, and abound in good works. "You, My disciples, I have planted in My evangelical ground; but all who do not bear fruit will be plucked up and cast into the fire. Remain in My presence. Live with Me as the branch on the vine, that you may produce fruits worthy of your holy vocation; for My Father, who is the heavenly Vine-dresser, will cut off all branches that bear no fruit." It is to you, O my soul, that these words are addressed. Weigh them in the scales of the sanctuary, and pass them not lightly over.

Affections.

O holy Founder, you love us more with less of other virtues and more humility, than with more of other virtues and less humility. O come with your powerful intercession, to help my weakness! O obtain for me sincere humility of heart, for pride and self-esteem have so dulled the ears of my soul, that these holy lessons have not penetrated it. O meek Jesus! O humble Jesus! if we are obliged to learn these di-

OUR SAVIOUR'S LESSONS. 95

vine virtues from Thee, with what degree of perfection should we not practise them? Everywhere I behold Thee meek and humble, in Thy life, in Thy conversation, in Thy works, and even in Thy death.

O my soul, will you not take to heart seriously this holy infancy and simplicity, since the Holy Ghost dwells not in deceitful souls, and they shall not dwell eternally in heaven. Withdraw, then, from me, worldly prudence, human respect, the opinion of creatures, love of self! Such considerations enter not into the mind of an innocent child, my model of simplicity. O Lord, if I possess this cherished virtue, Thou wilt take me lovingly into Thy divine arms, for the simple of heart are the children of love.

Little will it profit me, O divine Saviour! to have been planted in the fertile soil of holy religion; for if I bear not fruits worthy of life eternal, Thou wilt pluck me out. O, may this misfortune never happen to me! And in order that the grace of my vocation may not be in vain, may Thy divine presence be the sun and the dew which will cause me to produce works of life and salvation.

EIGHTEENTH MEDITATION.

THE MEANS BY WHICH THE RELIGIOUS SOUL RAVISHES THE HEART OF HER BELOVED.

I. Point.

CONSIDER that as God has sweetly drawn you away from the world, He wishes by a humble mutual exchange that you should ravish His Sacred Heart with love. What method will you adopt? Listen! He Himself teaches you: "My sister," He says, "thou hast ravished My Heart with one of thy eyes, and with one of thy hairs." Behold! by heroic works and great virtues you will gain the Heart of this Beloved; you will do so, likewise, by the practise of the little and lowly virtues.

II. Point.

Reflect that as the human body has only two eyes, but an abundance of hair, your Spouse displays incomparable mercy in allowing you to ravish His Heart with a single hair. Ah! at any moment you may possess that Divine Heart; for what are hairs but the ordinary observances, those little ceremonies, those daily virtues which we may practise at every turn? When you disregard them, you do not consider that you are neglecting to ravish the Heart of God. "If you would enter into life," said the meek Jesus to His apostles, "keep with fidelity all that I have taught you."

III. Point.

Reflect on the value the saints attached to the practice of these little virtues. They remembered that he who neglects little sins shall soon fall into greater. The small monastic observances are the hedge which preserves the religious life, like the vine of Our Saviour, from wild beasts, and whoever demolishes that hedge shall be bitten by the infernal serpent. Moreover, these minute observances are the habit of religion, which appears plain and without ornament. In short, the holy Founder remarked, that if he were in one of our convents, he would be so exact in all the little practices as thereby to ravish the Heart of God.

Affections.

O sovereign goodness of the great God, how adorable you are! Did a king ever give his vassals access to his cabinet that they might take from him his treasures? Yet at all times, O God of goodness, Thou dost teach me how I may obtain possession of Thy Heart and make it my own! Ah,

Lord! if it were only the martyrs that could ravish Thy Heart by their eyes and their blood, what would we do? But the mortified have the same privilege. If only they who convert nations, what would we do? Ah! they who speak humbly and lovingly of Thee, who inspire others to do good,—they have the same reward. If it were only conquerors of others, what would we do? But self-conquerors have the same happiness. Blessed forever be Thy sweet goodness!

O holy and little virtues, which grow like flowers at the foot of the cross of my Jesus, with holy solicitude I desire to cull you, that I may reverently present you to my Spouse. O my Jesus, preserve me from the reproach that Thou didst make to the Pharisees, saying that "they attended to small things, and neglected great ones." Grant me the grace to do the latter and omit not the former, in imitation of Thee, O Lord. Thou didst take little children into Thy arms through love and sweetness, but Thou didst not fail to carry sinners on Thy shoulders through mercy. Grant that I may carefully observe the silence of obligation, and that through devotion I may speak no useless words; that I may strictly obey my Superiors through a principle of duty, and willingly condescend to my equals through love.

O religion, most dear Mother, may it please God that I never divest myself of your holy habit, or break down the hedge which preserves you! My God, with Thy grace, I desire to observe all my obligations, but in the end to acknowledge myself a useless servant.

NINETEENTH MEDITATION.

THE LOVE OF OUR NEIGHBOR.

I. Point.

REFLECT that Our Saviour, beholding the hour of His death approaching, assembled His disciples in order to engrave upon their hearts His last will and testament. He said to them: "This is My commandment, that you love one another. By this they will know that you are My disciples, if you have love for one another."

II. Point.

Reflect that Our Saviour taught this love of our neighbor not only by words, but by His own adorable example. Wishing to die for love of all mankind, He gave Himself

LOVE OF OUR NEIGHBOR. 103

to us in the Most Blessed Sacrament, nay, even to Judas, whom He did not refuse to kiss, although He knew him to be His enemy. O my Saviour! Thy example confounds me. Alas! rarely am I willing to inconvenience myself, or give up my own wishes for the love of my neighbor, yet Thou teachest me at all times to love him in deed and in truth, and not alone in word. Thou dost assure me that I shall never enter Thy celestial temple, except by one gate, that of charity, which opens from two sides —the love of God and the love of the neighbor.

III. Point.

Reflect that Our Lord did not say: "Love some of your neighbors." No. His command comprehends them all. You will, therefore, bear unworthily the title of Religious, if this love is not perfect in you.

104 LOVE OF OUR NEIGHBOR.

If you do not feel love and gratitude toward those that do you good, you are ungrateful. If you do not love those that despise you, you are proud. If you do not love those that afflict you, you are impatient, etc. By all this you see that without this holy charity for the neighbor you have no virtue.

Affections.

Ah, Lord! if your servants are known by this holy mark of charity for the neighbor, I have great reason to fear, I who love myself so much, that I can scarcely resolve to abandon for even a little while my own interests for those of my dear neighbor. On all occasions, O heavenly Master, Thou offerest me Thy love as a model! My soul, let us consider in the presence of God, in what manner we should love our neighbors by following His example. Sweet Jesus!

LOVE OF OUR NEIGHBOR.

Thou didst undergo labor to acquire for them repose. Thou didst suffer ignominy in order to obtain for them glory. Behold, O my soul, what we must endeavor to do. O Lord! despoil me of self-love, that I may be able to imitate Thee!

From the bottom of my soul, sweet Jesus! I crave a favor of Thee, namely, that Thou wouldst grant me the grace always to put myself in the place of my neighbor, do unto him only that which I would wish him to do to me, and do unto him *all* that I would wish him to do to me. O Lord! if I look with an evil eye upon those that displease me, wilt Thou not withdraw from me Thy benign countenance? If I speak ill of my neighbor, wilt Thou not be silent toward me? Thou wilt speak no word to my soul. If I refuse him my services, Thou wilt deny me Thy graces.

God forbid that I should make exceptions in my love for my neighbor! O Lord! Thou wilt grant me Thy grace. Without regard to self, I will love Thee in my neighbor, and never will I love any one but in Thee and for Thee. Farewell, private friendships, particular affections! What! would you distract my soul with a diversity of objects, and withdraw my mind from its duty and its Rule? Come into my heart, O sweet religious union and holy community life, for it is you that the Lord blesses.

TWENTIETH MEDITATION.

THE GARDEN OF OLIVES.

I. Point.

CONTEMPLATE the God of majesty entering at night the Garden of Olives. He becomes pale, sadness oppresses Him. "Ah!" He exclaims, "My soul is sorrowful even unto death!" Prostrated in prayer, He says to His eternal Father: "Father, if it be possible let this chalice pass away, yet not My will, but Thine be done!" Three times He repeats the same prayer with such anguish and energy that a bloody sweat covers Him.

II. Point.

What is it that has drawn this sadness of death from the Soul of life? Doubtless, it is love which has loaded Him with the sins of men and which wishes for their sake to experience the fear and dread of the inferior part of the soul. What dost Thou say, O my Jesus—that Thy soul is sorrowful even unto death? Alas! was it not Thou who once said to the apostles, that Thou hadst a great desire to be baptized with the baptism of Thy Passion? Yes, those were Thine own words. But, as St. Augustine remarks, having been created by power and authority, Thou didst wish to ransom us in weakness and suffering.

III. Point.

Reflect that the eternal Father heard His Son for His reverence, says St. Paul; and as to the Benjamin of His Heart, He sent Him the cup of torments by one of His angelic servants. Our sweet Jesus then received the chalice so lovingly that He resolved to drink it even to the dregs, and to allow neither affronts nor confusion nor sorrow to overcome Him. To this end, He went Himself to meet His enemies.

Affections.

O Jesus! afflicted even unto death, what can I say to Thee? Eve tasted in the garden the sweetness of the fruit; but as for Thee, my Redeemer, love made Thee taste the bitterness of the pain due to her vain pleasure. Ah, what great secrets are enclosed in that garden! Dear Spouse, when Thou wast sorrowful and afflicted, Thou wast far away from Thy most intimate friends; but when I undergo the slightest annoyance, I run to creatures for sympathy. Thou didst address Thyself to Thy Father with such resignation and perseverance, that Thou didst sweat blood; but I cannot watch even one hour with Thee. I weary of prayer,

110 *THE GARDEN OF OLIVES.*

my resignation is only by halves. Henceforth, O Lord, I shall adopt Thy language: "Not my will, O Father, but Thine be done!"

O Jesus, love stronger than death loaded Thee in the garden with sorrows, with my sins, with my infidelities, with my resistance to Thy graces, and love made Thee grieve over my wretchedness! My sweet Jesus, if such apprehensions could exist in the inferior part of Thy soul whilst contemplating death, what should I think, criminal that I am, on beholding Thee, O King of innocence? Ah, I should be convinced that Thy death acquired life for Thy children, as Thy weakness obtained strength for them.

O creatures! prevent not my drinking the chalice of afflictions that my heavenly Father sends me, for I desire to render myself conformable to Jesus suffering!

THE GARDEN OF OLIVES.

Take, O humble Jesus, take this chalice that the Father sends Thee. Ah, my soul! what is it that the Father sends to His Son? Consolation? No, rather an increase of torments. Was it not His consolation to do in all things the will of His Father? This it was that strengthened Him, so that instead of retarding Him, He goes forward to meet His sufferings. O creatures! whoever you may be, do not prevent me from accepting the chalice that my Father offers me.

TWENTY-FIRST MEDITATION.

THE LOVE OF OUR SAVIOUR IN THE MIDST OF HIS LABORS.

I. Point.

REFLECT that the eternal Father so loved the world that He gave to it His only Son; and the Son so loved the will of His Father that, knowing He wished to save human nature, and considering not the abjection and misery thereby entailed, He voluntarily offered an enormous price for its ransom; namely, His own blood, His sweat, and His life.

II. Point.

Our Saviour, urged by His love, bows to the will of His Father, and offers Him-

THE LOVE OF OUR SAVIOUR. 113

self for the redemption of the world. In each mystery of His Passion, He exclaims: "O My Father! human nature would be sufficiently redeemed by one of My tears; but that would not suffice for the reverence I bear Thy holy will, that would not satisfy My love. I long to undergo My agony in the garden, I long to be struck, to be crowned with thorns, to be reduced to so pitiable a state as to become like unto a leper without shape or comeliness."

III. Point.

Our meek Jesus was scourged, crowned with thorns, condemned, mocked, and ignored, because He was destined and consecrated to bear opprobrium and ignominy as punishments consequent on our sins. He became a holocaust for sin, being, as it were, accursed, exiled from His eternal Father, and abandoned by Him.

Affections.

My soul, dwell for the future amid the thorns and the scourges of the Saviour. There, like a nightingale, humbly sigh: Live Jesus, who wishes to die that my soul may live! O eternal Father, what return can the world make to Thee for the gift Thou hast bestowed upon it in Thy only-begotten Son? To redeem man, a thing as vile as I am, He delivered Himself; and, ingrate that I am, I play the miser, giving not even my nothingness to Him who has given me His all!

Ah! if I am the spouse of Jesus crucified and suffering, I must throughout my whole life consider it an immense favor to clothe myself with His livery; namely, the nails, the thorns, and the lance. Remember, my soul, that the feast of His nuptials is gall and vinegar. O King of glory! it is too great an honor to drink with Thee the chalice of suffering. Never let it happen that I refuse this beverage; for, as David says: "It is, O God, the drink of Thy well-beloved."

O Religious, who have undertaken to follow Jesus crucified, know that you should be stripped of your own affections, as He was of His sacred garment. O my God! I deceive myself if I wish to gather the myrrh of Thy mortifications with one hand and the miserable gratifications of the earth with the other. Guard me from this misfortune, my beloved Jesus, and make me walk with Thee to glory by the road of sorrow.

TWENTY-SECOND MEDITATION.

OUR SAVIOUR ON THE CROSS.

I. Point.

REFLECT upon what St. Augustine says, that "Isaac was immolated by his father's will where Jesus was afterward crucified, and that the cross of the Saviour was planted on the sepulchre of Adam." It was most appropriate that the Physician should be raised up from the couch of the sick man, and that the divine mercy should descend upon the place where pride fell. In order, therefore, that our blessed Saviour should shed His blood upon the ashes of the first transgressor, and that the soul which was, at the Last Day, to animate those same ashes might be cleansed of sin, the cross upon which Jesus was nailed was planted on the tomb of Adam.

II. Point.

Contemplate the divine Saviour extended and elevated on this cross, as on a funeral pile of honor. Ah! it was then that, as a great bishop, He offered the perfect sacrifice to His Father; it was then that He turned thoughts of special love upon us. "O My eternal Father! I take upon Myself all the sins of this, My daughter. I load Myself with them in order to suffer death, that she may be forgiven. I die, that she may live. I long to be crucified, that she may be glorified." O sovereign love of the Heart of Jesus! what heart is capable of devoutly blessing Thee?

III. Point.

Behold, whilst the Jews with hearts of iron and stone surround the cross, our meek

Jesus, on the contrary, as David says, "has a Heart liquefied with love in the midst of His breast." And like that admirable bird which attracts to itself the jaundice of man, and dies in order to heal him, this wonderful Bird of paradise, our sweet Jesus, who was never stained with the jaundice of sin, is fastened to the cross to draw into Himself the poison from man, His beloved friend. He gladly dies in order to give life to our poor human nature.

Affections.

" O God ! " I repeat with St. Augustine, lamenting the ingratitude of men, " is it possible that man knows that Thou didst die for him, and yet he does not live for Thee ? " And with St. Francis: " Alas, O Jesus ! my sweet Jesus ! Thou didst die of love, and no one thinks of it ! " My sweet Redeemer, never was the misery of Adam so poisonous to us, as Thy clemency is powerful to save us. O obedient Jesus! obedient even unto the death of the cross, be Thou the Repairer of all my acts of disobedience! May Thy precious blood sink into the deepest wounds of my soul, for it is the medicine of my salvation!

O free will of my heart! how desirable to be fastened to the cross of our divine Saviour in order to die to self, to offer self as a holocaust to the Lord! Never forget, O my soul, that your Congregation is spiritually founded on Mount Calvary for the service of this crucified Lover, in imitation of whom we must crucify the senses, imagination, aversions, passions, and humors for the love of the heavenly Father.

O innocent Jesus, who didst die for my iniquity, grant that I may no longer live but for Thy goodness! Like the mystical serpent, love has elevated Thee on high!

If I do not look upon Thee, my sweet Physician, I shall not deserve to be cured. Therefore, O Lord! may my eyes be constantly fixed on Thy sufferings, and my heart riveted to Thy goodness! Jesus, by Thy pierced hands, pardon my evil deeds! By Thy pierced feet, grant me forgiveness of my transgressions!

TWENTY-THIRD MEDITATION.

THE FIRST FIVE WORDS THAT OUR SAVIOUR SPOKE ON THE CROSS.

I. Point.

REFLECT that our meek Jesus, on beholding His enemies around Him, exclaimed: "Father, forgive them, for they know not what they do!" O what perfect charity! Our Saviour not being able to justify the sin of His wicked executioners, casts about for the most plausible excuse for them, namely, ignorance. Moreover, it was on this holy cross, with a heart so full of love for men, that Jesus, to the thief who merely asked Him to remember him, gave a solemn promise of paradise. Oh, what a fearful thing is the fall of those that are called to a high vocation! Judas, the apostle, was lost through pride; the thief humbles himself, and he is saved.

II. Point.

Behold St. John and the most blessed Virgin at the foot of the cross, at the feet of their Beloved, who, seeing His Mother overwhelmed with grief, said to her: "Woman, behold your son!" namely, John; and to John: "Behold your Mother!" O admirable Mother! was it not fitting that your heart should be thoroughly accustomed to the language of love, and should comprehend its meaning? You understood that He gave you as a Mother to His spouse the Church, to which He gave birth on the cross, says St. Augustine. O incomparable thought! As soon as Jesus had pronounced this third word, the sun, as if touched with lively sorrow, withdrew

OUR SAVIOUR'S FIRST WORDS.

his light, and darkness spread over the whole earth.

III. Point.

Hark! After three hours of silence, our sweet Saviour cries out: "My God, My God, why hast Thou forsaken Me?" The inferior part of His soul was so abandoned, so crushed with sorrow, so beset with woe, that, in order to console us in our weaknesses, He complained to His Father; but to prove that the superior part longed for these sufferings, He exclaimed: "I thirst." He alluded not to corporal thirst. Let us believe, my soul, that He had a burning thirst, burning for the salvation of those that thirsted so ardently for His ruin. O poor people! You ask Jesus to come down from the cross; but He takes care not to do so. He thirsts too ardently for your salvation, which He must obtain by His death on it.

Affections.

O kind Saviour, what tenderness of heart Thou dost teach me for my neighbor—that I should even excuse those who crucified my Spouse! Ah! I will say with the Apostle: "If they had known Him, they would not have crucified the God of glory." But beware, my soul, lest the disorderly passions that closed their eyes blind your own. O my Saviour, Thou dost excuse Thy executioners, even in the act of sinning, and scarcely can we forget a contradiction long after receiving it, scarcely can we look kindly upon those who have ever so slightly displeased us.

O holy and most devoted Mother! receive John as your son, that is to say, receive the children of the Church as your children, and we shall henceforth be permitted to call you Mother. O Jesus! Thou didst will to die naked and despoiled of all things, even to the giving of Thine own dear Mother to us.

O sweet Saviour! it was by no means to offend against holy indifference, that Thou didst utter a complaint to Thy Father. It was to console us in our trials, and make us realize the actual sorrow and anguish of Thy blessed soul, for not the sorrows of death alone, but also the thirst of love consumed Thee, and made Thee long ardently for our salvation. Ah! am I not an ingrate, if I complain in my little trials, since I behold the only Son of God thirsting to undergo suffering for me? If such a Father abandons the inferior part of the soul of such a Son, why not the soul of a miserable slave?

TWENTY-FOURTH MEDITATION.

THE BLESSED VIRGIN STANDING AT THE FOOT OF THE CROSS.

I. Point.

CONSIDER the most blessed Virgin, in all constancy standing at the foot of the cross of her Son. Ah! what do you seek, O Mother of Life, in this place of Calvary and of death? Truly, not for joy, but for your dear Son. With your whole maternal heart you desire to be united to Him; therefore, do I behold you in this place of Calvary, bound and exposed with your divine Son.

II. Point.

Love attracted all the pains, torments, wounds, the whole Passion of Our Redeemer into the heart of His most blessed Mother. The same nails that crucified the body of the divine Son crucified the heart of the Mother. The thorns of His crown pierced her soul so that she could truly exclaim: " My Beloved is a bouquet of myrrh to me, but so loved that He remains between my breasts, that is, in my breast, in the centre of my heart."

III. Point.

Contemplate the most blessed Virgin as a mystical bee, extracting honey from the wounds of the Lion of the tribe of Juda, immolated, torn to pieces, and lacerated on the cross. " O Child of the cross," said she, " let us glory in Thy admirable mission which the world does not comprehend. O all you who pass through this world, behold how amiable is the death of my Son, since it is the sovereign outcome of His love. Ah! my Jesus must die that the human race may not perish."

Affections.

Your holy Abbess, O religious souls, is not on the mountain of Thabor, but on the hill of Calvary, where she beholds only opprobrium, impotence, the lance, the nails, and darkness. O Mother of devoted love, the waves of affliction cannot extinguish your charity, though one tiny drop of trouble and contradiction causes me to take refuge behind my suffering and beloved Jesus.

Most blessed Virgin, as you were a vessel of election, the greatest, the most capable, the most worthy in the world, you were also, more than any other, filled with bitterness, with the beverage of anguish which your Beloved drank in this place of torments. Ah! what does this teach me, if not to receive tribulations as something that I share with our Spouse? O Mother most pure, you call to us, saying: "Come, my daughters, let your hearts be like empty vessels, and my Son will pour into them the dew with which His forehead is covered, and the drops of the night of His Passion with which His head is adorned. He will turn them for you into pearls of consolation." My sweet Mother! obtain for me the grace henceforth to receive all occasions of humiliation, of suffering, and of abjection, as tiny drops of blood trickling from that precious head.

O mystical Bee, grant me the grace that, in the hive of my cloister and in the small apartment of my heart, I may, in imitation of you, make practical use of the honey gathered from the sacred wounds of Our Saviour. Depart from me, earthly cravings! The gall of my King is sweeter to me than the honeycomb. O Mother of sorrows and fountain of love, never permit me to withdraw from the hallowed foot of the adorable cross.

TWENTY-FIFTH MEDITATION.

THE DEATH OF OUR SAVIOUR ON THE CROSS.

I. Point.

REFLECT that it was on the cross that the eternal Son gave the kiss of love to His heavenly Father in favor of mankind. It was then and there that the Father perceived a sweet odor coming from the garments of His Son, that is to say, from His holy humanity. "Ah!" He exclaimed, "the odor of My Son resembles that of a field blooming and plentiful." Yes; for Jesus, Flower of the fields, having been crushed beneath the press of the cross, gave forth a perfume which rejoiced God, ravished the angels, and redeemed mankind.

II. Point.

Our Saviour cried out: "All is consummated," the redemption of the world is accomplished. My Father, I remit My spirit into Thy hands. I have already given Thee My body, My sweat, My blood; nothing now remains but the soul that animates this mutilated body. O My Father, I remit it into Thy hands, do with it as it shall please Thee. Grant only that Thy will be accomplished, whether Thou desirest My soul still to remain in this body, or that I should breathe it out into Thy hands.

III. Point.

Reflect that our meek Jesus sees that His Father desires His departure. Death not being able to enter into Him who holds the keys of life and death, love opened the door to death, so that it might destroy His precious body. And Jesus, bowing His head

THE DEATH OF OUR SAVIOUR.

in order to give the kiss of peace to His blessed Mother and to His nascent Church, expired through His own election of love. Then, O God, sepulchres were opened, the earth trembled, and the veil of the Temple was rent in twain; all things rendered homage to the Conqueror of death.

Affections.

O Jesus of Nazareth, King of the Jews, how precious is the sacred blood that flows from Thy most pure body! Thou art alone, no one assists Thee to turn the heavy winepress, nevertheless Thy sacred body, the divine garment of Thy soul, is crimson with its own blood, because Thou art in the day of Thy vintage. O eternal Father, behold the face of Thy Christ, and have pity on His brethren! Sweet Jesus, mutilated, trodden upon, lacerated in all Thy members, what confusion for me not to wish that I may be torn to pieces by mortification! Nevertheless, it is only by that means that I shall give forth the sweet liquor of virtue. O religious souls, be ashamed to call yourselves members of Jesus Christ, if you are not willing to suffer with Jesus Christ; for it is too great an indignity to see delicate and sensual members under a head crowned with thorns.

O dear Jesus, I know that torments grievous enough to cause the death of an entire world were Thine, nevertheless they were insufficient to make Thee die. It was expedient that Thou shouldst Thyself remit Thy soul into the hands of Thy Father, all things having been fulfilled. From this I learn the quintessence of the spiritual life, namely, perfect abandonment into the hands of the heavenly Father. Ah, may I often pronounce these blessed words: " Father, I remit my spirit into Thy hands.

Do unto me this or that according to Thy will! My Superiors, I have accomplished your commands, laborious and abject though they be. I abandon myself into your hands that, if it so please you, I may begin anew." Happy shall I be if I live in this manner!

Incline Thy head, O my divine King, and call upon death to give me life. O why is death feared? My Jesus has endured it! Ah, Jesus, God of life, grant me the grace at the hour of my death to remit my soul into Thy hands, for Thou art my true Father! Wither away with love and sorrow, O my soul, on beholding Jesus dead for your sins. Depart not from the holy mount of Calvary, until you have entombed the beloved Spouse in your heart.

TWENTY-SIXTH MEDITATION.

THE JOY AND HAPPINESS THAT THE DEVOUT SOUL EXPERIENCES IN THE CROSS.

I. Point.

STRIKING my breast at the foot of the cross of my sweet Jesus, I will exclaim, "Here is truly the Son of God!" Never may I glory in myself, nor in the world, nor in anything whatever. Let Jonas rejoice under the shadow of his ivy, let Abraham prepare beneath the tree a feast for the angels, let Ismael cry under the tree of the desert, let Elias be fed in solitude beneath the juniper-tree; as for us, we wish for no other joy than that of the cross, no other drink than the blood which flows therefrom, no other nourishment than the fruit of life suspended on it.

II. Point.

Consider how venerable is this cross. "Ah!" exclaimed David, "adore the footprints of God." And what shall we say of the cross that has been the bed, the seat, the throne, of that same God? Jacob adored the rod of Joseph, and Esther kissed the rod of her husband Assuerus. Oh! then, with what reverence should the devout soul kiss the cross, the true royal sceptre of her dear Jesus! She should say with David: "O all you preach, and say that the Lord reigns by the wood."

III. Point.

Consider how exceedingly the dearest friends of God have loved the cross. The most blessed Virgin, sacred Sulamitess, ascended this palm at every moment in order to cull its fruits; St. Peter had no other strength, St. Paul no other glory, St. John no other refuge, St. Andrew no other sweetness; and as to our Father, St. Francis de Sales, he protested that, if he knew that a single fibre of his heart was not stamped with the cross, he would pluck it out.

Affections.

O most holy cross, honored by the sacred members of my Saviour, you are the royal gate that conducts to the temple of holiness, outside of which we shall never find it. O religious souls! contemplate profoundly the wounds that Our Lord suffered on the cross, and learn that vain and foolish is the heart that perches on any other tree. I salute you, O holy cross, standard of salvation, palm of life, sword by which the devil was annihilated, medicine of immortality, protector of the present life, pledge of life eternal, sacred sign of Chris-

HAPPINESS IN THE CROSS. 139

tians, trophy of our King, Jesus! O dear and desirable cross! receive me within your venerable arms.

O Jesus, my Spouse! in kissing and embracing Thy own cross, Thou didst embrace all our little crosses, thus to render them more amiable. O little crosses, little trials, little repugnances, humiliations, trifling though you be, my Jesus has seen, has kissed, has sanctified you. Why, then, throughout the journey of this life, should I not have recourse to Thy transpierced Heart? At every step we meet with crosses. If my flesh trembles at the sight of them, my heart loves them. Yes, I love you, little and great crosses, interior and exterior, corporal and spiritual, though I am unworthy of the honor of your shadow.

Whence, alas! comes the misfortune that reverence for the cross has grown so cold? The primitive Christians and lovers of

140 HAPPINESS IN THE CROSS.

Jesus always made this sign of life with great veneration, when eating and drinking, standing and sitting. "When thou goest out, when thou dost enter the house, when thou bringest a light, cover thyself with the sacred sign of the cross, and evils dare not approach thee," says an ancient writer. O holy Lover of the cross, grant that, following Thy example, I may love the crucifixion of the body and of the heart! O holy cross! be to me a most amiable chain, and a rampart upon my breast!

TWENTY-SEVENTH MEDITATION.

THE RESURRECTION OF OUR LORD.

I. Point.

REFLECT that, after a deluge of torments, of sadness, and of sorrow had been inflicted on Our Saviour, He arose from the tomb by His own power, and early in the morning, beauteous, resplendent, subtile, agile, and all-glorious, He went to visit His most blessed Mother. Rejoice, O holy Mother! Behold your dear Jesus more triumphant than ever. Behold the temple that the Jews had demolished, raised up again. Behold, the sign of Jonas has come. Behold your dear Joseph alive.

II. Point.

Reflect that joy was immense in the Ark

of Noe when the dove returned, bearing an olive branch as a sign that the flood had ceased and that God had bestowed the blessing of peace. But, O God! with what delight was not the band of apostles ravished, when they saw the sacred humanity of the Saviour, resuscitated and glorious, returning to them, bearing in His mouth the olive branch of holy and acceptable peace! "*Pax vobis*," He said. This is the indubitable sign of the cessation of the waters of the Father's anger; here is the sign of reconciliation of man with God.

III. Point.

Consider how necessary it was that the benign Saviour should visit His disciples. Their faith, their hope, and their charity were wavering. It was Magdalen who had gone forth to embalm Him. The disciples of Emmaus said: " We had hoped; " and the

RESURRECTION OF OUR LORD.

rest of them looked upon the words of the holy women as dreams. Behold why Our Saviour, fearing their peril, like a good Master, came to strengthen them. " I am indeed Myself, beloved disciples. See My hands, My feet, and the wound of My side."

Affections.

O blessed and faithful Virgin, how sweet to your maternal heart was this joyful news: "Your Son is alive!" O holy daughters of Sion! dry your tears, behold, your Beloved has come! Since you have drunk the cup of His sorrows, as His Benjamin, He will give you the first and the greatest share in the joy of His glory. My soul, reverence in silence the triumphant Son of our comforted Mother.

O sweet Jesus! if my interior was well ordered and prepared for Thy coming, Thou wouldst address to me the consoling words:

"Peace be to you!" Alas, my heart! if we had once received the peace of Jesus, the world could no longer disturb us. Holy peace, sung by the angels at the birth of the Saviour, and bequeathed by Him at His Resurrection, be forever in my heart! Now I firmly believe that my Redeemer liveth, and that at the Last Day I shall rise again.

From this thought I make the determined resolution never to profane my body. As I shall not flatter it, since it must perish, I shall also guard it as destined to rise again in glory. For as my eyes shall eternally behold Our Saviour, I shall withdraw them from vain and useless objects. As I shall receive the kiss of the glorious Spouse, I shall not allow indecent, irreligious, quarrelsome words, or words of murmuring and excuse to pass my lips. I shall observe similar circumspection with regard to my other senses.

Come, O my Beloved, strengthen my faith, for confiding in Thy power honors Thy Father; my hope, because it is established on Thy redemption; my charity, since it embraces the goodness of the Holy Ghost. O dear Lover, what wilt Thou ask while showing Thy wounds, if not, "Have you need of strength? Behold My hands. Do you want heart? Here is My Sacred Heart. Are you a dove? Here is the cleft of the corner-stone, come, repose therein." Lord, I have need of all this, and still more. I am sick and a prisoner, but I go to Thee, and there I find my medicine and my salvation.

TWENTY-EIGHTH MEDITATION.

THE ASCENSION OF OUR LORD.

I. Point.

REFLECT that the Blessed Virgin, on the day of the Ascension of her Son, could not, indeed, apply to Him this passage of the canticle of love: "Flee away, my Beloved, to the eternal hills, filled with an eternal sweetness;" but "Be Thou like a roe that turns frequently to see those that it leaves behind."

II. Point.

Behold the holy band assembled on the mountain of Olives. Our glorious Redeemer blesses them all; then, in the chariot of His power and omnipotence, He ascends triumphantly into heaven. " O," exclaimed the Blessed Virgin, " behold how beautiful is my Beloved! How holy is the cross which He carries as a trophy of victory! It is of incorruptible wood." The Lord has crowned our Conqueror with the glory of His Resurrection and Ascension; this thought should ravish the whole world with His praise.

III. Point.

As this generous assembly kept their eyes riveted on our sweet Jesus who ascended on high, a cloud hid Him from their gaze; nevertheless, they did not cease to look after Him, until the angels, the servants of our King, said to them: " Why stand ye here looking up to heaven? This Jesus whom ye have seen taken up to heaven will come again to judge the living and the dead." Then the holy company returned to Jerusalem, whilst the victorious Prince, who led captivity captive, was seated at the right hand of the Father, placing His faithful servants on the thrones that Lucifer and the rebel angels had forfeited. O God, what a favor to mankind, what happiness to the angels, what jubilation in the heavenly Jerusalem!

Affections.

O most blessed Virgin! who dost invite your Beloved to ascend on high, would that we were despoiled of all self-interest! The other daughters of Sion call Him with a loud voice, and beg Him not to leave them; but you, O chaste Dove! you seek the glory of your Son, and in this consist your joy and felicity. Yes, O my Lord, go to the eternal hills, but cast Thy holy and merciful looks upon us at every instant.

"Alas, O Lord!" says St. Augustine,

ASCENSION OF OUR LORD.

" how deeply do I grieve at not being present on the mount of Olives to kiss the holes made by the nails, and to bathe with sweetest tears of joy the wounds of Thy precious body!" O my Jesus! I was absent and far away when Thou didst ascend into paradise. With hands raised to heaven, Thou didst bless Thy disciples, and I was not there; the angels consoled them, and I heard no word of comfort. What shall I do now? Where shall I seek Thee? No, there is no more joy in my heart; my soul refuses all consolation, except from Thee. O unutterable sweetness! May my conversation be in heaven, where my Jesus reigns in His glory!

O angels of peace! blame me not if I always look on high; for where my Jesus is, there is my treasure. By sending His disciples into Jerusalem, where they had orders to expect the Paraclete, you teach me at all times to perform promptly what my Beloved ordains. O holy company delivered from Limbo, whom Jesus establishes in His glory, remember, like Elias, to let your mantle fall on your servant. Drop upon my poor soul the mantle of faith and the veil of hope, you who need only the precious robe of charity.

TWENTY-NINTH MEDITATION.

THE DESCENT OF THE HOLY GHOST.

I. Point.

CHOSEN souls, enter humbly into the cenacle, where the glorious Virgin, the holy apostles, the faithful disciples, and the devout women are assembled in prayer, in recollection, in faith, in hope, expecting their good Master to fulfil His promise, and that you all may be clothed with virtue from on high. Turn away from distractions, in order to receive this perfect gift from the Father of lights, for God will never pour upon you His mercies if He does not find you interiorly recollected and separated from the world. Do you not see that this happy company, though in Jerusalem, remains retired, as it were, in a desert?

II. Point.

Ten days after Our Saviour had ascended on high, and after His beloved had been prepared by silence, fraternity, and prayer, suddenly there came a sound from heaven, as of a mighty wind. It filled the whole house in which they were assembled, and there appeared to them tongues, as it were of fire, that sat upon every one of them. Oh! even in our own day, God imparts His gifts. We have only to desire them in order to receive them.

III. Point.

Reflect how greatly the eternal Father loves the holy Church, since He has enriched it with His own treasures. Not satisfied with giving it His Son and His image,

DESCENT OF THE HOLY GHOST.

He still further bestows upon it His Holy Spirit, so that, as the Holy Ghost overshadowed the Virgin, of whose pure blood Jesus was to be born, in order to become the Father of the Church, so in like manner does the Holy Spirit descend to embrace it, lately sprung from the blood of the Saviour.

Affections.

Oh! who will give me the grace to maintain interior peace, far from the distractions of the world, so that I may in silence expect the coming of the Holy Ghost? O blessed Virgin! O glorious apostles! obtain for me your devotion, that I may persevere in prayer in order that, should Our Lord delay to come, I may await in patience. I know, O my God! that Thou wilt not leave me an orphan, but if I continue to obey Thee, Thou wilt send me Thy Spirit of truth.

Come, Holy Spirit, fill our hearts with the fire of Thy charity. Come, Father of the poor, come, Giver of gifts, Light of hearts! O sweet Jesus, wishing to promulgate Thy law, Thou didst cast upon Thy disciples tongues of fire, showing clearly thereby that evangelical preaching is wholly destined for the inflaming of hearts with heavenly love. O Holy Spirit, who didst bring fire upon earth, what dost Thou wish except that it may burn? Once more I conjure Thee to fill my heart with the fire of Thy charity, of that charity, I repeat, which endures all things, which believes all things, and which is not envious.

O holy Church of the living God, how rich you are! The blessed laborers in your vineyard are filled with the Holy Spirit. He transforms them into fire, love, and zeal.

DESCENT OF THE HOLY GHOST. 155

They are vessels full of the wine of the Spouse, and so disgusted with terrestrial things, that they consider themselves happy to live ever after in anguish, in persecution, and in a state of death for their dear Jesus. O Holy Spirit! if I receive Thee without resistance, doubtless Thou wilt produce within me great effects. I shall speak only of the marvels of God; I shall seek but His glory and my own abasement; I shall esteem myself favored to suffer opprobrium for the name of the Lord.

THIRTIETH MEDITATION.

THE PRESENCE OF GOD.

I. Point.

REFLECT that heaven and earth are full of the majesty of God, who is in all things and everywhere, by His essence, His presence, and His power. O how can we forget a truth so infallible and so encouraging? "Oh!" exclaimed Moses to animate his people, "there is no nation that has its gods so near it as we have, for our God is always with us. His eyes see us continually, His ears are lovingly inclined to hear us in all places."

II. Point.

Reflect that attention to the divine presence is an efficacious means to arrive at

THE PRESENCE OF GOD.

perfection. It was one of the first precepts that God gave to His servant Abraham: "Walk before Me, and be perfect." O Lord, what else didst Thou say to me in placing me in this holy convent, except, "My daughter, walk always in My presence, and you will attain perfection! Think on Me in all your ways, and I will conduct your steps."

III. Point.

Reflect into what an abuse and misfortune the soul falls that is forgetful of this divine presence! The two old men of Babylon turned their eyes away from heaven, in order not to remember their sins. "You are mad," says David, "if you say: 'The God of Jacob does not see me, the God of Israel watches not.' For His eyes behold all upon the face of the earth. He sees and contemplates all that is done upon it; He sounds hearts, He foresees thoughts; nothing escapes Him, His eye observes all things."

Affections.

O sweet Jesus, my Saviour and my God! assuredly I know that if I ascend up to heaven, Thou art there; if I descend into hell, there I find Thee; if my spirit flies to the extremity of the seas, and descends into the abysses, there I meet Thee. Therefore, why shall I not serve Thee everywhere? Why shall I not pray to Thee in all places, since in all places, my Beloved, Thou dost listen to me? O sovereign King! how happy are they who belong entirely to Thee! Thou dost give them audience at all hours. Who will obtain for me the grace that in all things and everywhere I may forget myself by the constant remembrance of Thee, who art more present to me than I am to myself. The further I withdraw from myself, the nearer I approach to Thee.

Wherefore, alas! is this disorder? I am called to walk before the Lord and to be perfect; but, on the contrary, I walk after my own appetites, my self-will, and my self-love; thus do I annihilate all perfection. O my soul! henceforth in all your actions you should look up to Him who sits at the right hand of the Father, invisible to our senses, but present to the heart, in which He desires to reign as He does in heaven.

O foolish and ungrateful spouse! dare you hereafter voluntarily turn away from your Beloved, in order to occupy yourself with the miserable amusements of earth? Ah! it is in His presence, it is before His eyes, that you are wanting in fidelity; nothing is concealed from the great Spectator who dwells on high. O God, searcher of hearts, may all my thoughts and my desires be directed to Thee!

THIRTY-FIRST MEDITATION.

THE PROVIDENCE OF GOD.

I. Point.

REFLECT that God's love for us is so great that He employs His wisdom, His power, and His goodness to conduct us to our end by means most suitable and effectual. Not only does His providence watch over the most important things of our salvation, but even over the most trifling events of our life. A hair of our head does not fall without His providence, and He knows even the number of them. Without His permission, neither men nor demons dare touch one of them.

II. Point.

Reflect that Divine Providence does all

for us with weight, number, and measure, says the Holy Scripture. Behold, then, the obligation we are under of leaving to Him the care of ourselves! Let us not consider what may happen to us, whether good, bad, or indifferent: whether it will elate us, or whether it will overwhelm us with anguish. Let us behold all events in the providence of God who, with incomprehensible love, employs His wisdom, power, and goodness in the guidance of so small a creature, in order to make it arrive at blessedness.

III. Point.

See how offended God is when we withdraw from the hands of His sweet providence, in order to conduct ourselves according to our own caprice! O how displeased He was with the children of Israel for having committed that fault! Abandoning His sweet providence, they wished to have a king to govern them, and they became wretched.

Affections.

O eternal Father! Thy providence governs all things. It is, indeed, strange that, being children of a Father who watches over us with so vigilant an eye, we should have any other solicitude than to serve and love Him well. "Ah!" said St. Francis de Sales, "my soul has no other refuge than the holy providence of God. O my God, Thou hast taught me this lesson from my youth, and forever shall I proclaim Thy marvels."

I adore Thee, O sovereign Wisdom, Power, and Goodness, who so lovingly directs all the moments of my life. O religious souls! our true to-morrow is Divine Providence. Behold the lilies of the fields, they neither sow nor do they spin, and the sweet providence of our heavenly Father clothes them better than Solomon was clothed in all his glory. O my God! I desire henceforth to hold in great esteem all that may happen to me. No, I shall not say that I have many afflictions, mortifications, and trials, for Thou hast counted their number. I shall not consider them too heavy, for Thou hast weighed them, as well as the strength that Thou dost give me with which to support them. I shall not say that they last too long a time, for Thou hast estimated their value.

O my Saviour, I wish no longer to interfere, I desire only to be conducted by Thee. The Shepherd who guides me is the Lord omnipotent. Nothing shall ever induce me to leave Him; no, never do I wish to meddle in what concerns me. Let Him make choice of my abode, my employment, my consolation, my humiliations, my health, my sickness, my death, my salvation. I desire only to follow His guidance, and to leave myself absolutely to Him.

THIRTY-SECOND MEDITATION.

THE WILL OF GOD.

I. Point.

REFLECT that since our salvation depends on the will of God, it is not to be doubted that all our perfection, all our happiness likewise rest thereon. Ah, how happy and peaceful will be the heart that, by love and total submission, realizes in all things that the divine will is good, pleasant, and perfect!

II. Point.

Reflect that the will of God is the sovereign queen of the universe. Nothing is done but in obedience to it. It ordains everything except sin, and we should regard all in this blessed will, without ever attempting to ascribe secondary causes. O how happy would religious souls be, if they considered all things in this happy source, and if they received all events as coming from His holy will! In all circumstances we should endeavor to hear these words of Habacuc, addressed to the Prophet Daniel: "Take what the Lord sends thee."

III. Point.

Reflect that the eternal Son of God came upon earth to teach the submission and reverence due the divine will, not only in so far as He said that He came not to do His own will, but that of His Father, but furthermore by His resignation: "Father, if it be possible, let this chalice pass away; nevertheless, Thy will, not Mine, be done." This good Master, moreover, teaches us to ask daily that the will of God may be done

THE WILL OF GOD. 167

on earth as it is in heaven. Finally, He concluded the whole course of His mortal life by the surrender of Himself to the will and disposition of His eternal Father: "My Father, I remit My spirit into Thy hands."

Affections.

O holy and divine will of my God! since the true characteristic and infallible mark of the daughters of my holy Congregation is to see you and to follow you in all things, I wish most earnestly to undertake this blessed exercise. O sweet will, how shall I know you in order that I may follow you? It is, indeed, good for me to adhere to Thee, O my God. I behold Thy will in Thy commandments. If I observe them, I shall be loved by Thee and by Thy Father. I recognize it in my rules, my vows, and observances, and therefore I shall endeavor to observe them carefully, for Thou hast said: "Vow ye, and pay to the Lord, your God." I know it in the direction of my Superiors, for God has said: "Be subject to your Superiors, and obey them; he who hears them, hears Me." I shall recognize it in treating with my neighbors. Whatsoever you wish your brother to do to you, do to him in like manner. In short, as I behold this divine will in all things, I shall by God's grace strive to honor it, and I shall follow it in every event of my life.

Ah! self-will, it is time for you to die, since I no longer desire to live but in the will of my God. I wish to follow it as my princess and mistress. Let it be inscribed in large characters on the first page of the book of my soul. My own judgment, no longer shall you be permitted to discern, to discourse, or to see; it is sufficient for you to submit yourself wholly to the divine dispensation. O my God! conduct me according to Thy will. Make me suffer from cold, from heat, from light, from darkness, in my labors and in my repose. If Thou dost conduct me even to the gates of death, under Thy guidance I shall not fear.

Yes, O heavenly Father, may Thy will be done on earth, where consolations are rare and trials innumerable! Take as a daily practice, O my soul, to say when something disturbs you, "Let not my will, but that of my God be accomplished."

THIRTY-THIRD MEDITATION.

DETACHMENT AND THE CONCLUSION OF THE RETREAT.

I. Point.

REFLECT what a favor God has bestowed upon you in this retreat, by giving you so many good inspirations and lights for your welfare. All should be directed to this one end, total self-detachment, so that you may hereafter be able to say truly and efficaciously: "Naked came I from the womb of my mother, and naked shall I return thither. The Lord gave [me life], the Lord hath taken [it] away. Blessed be His holy name!"

II. Point.

Consider the happy condition in which

perfect detachment from all things places the soul, namely, that she sighs only for her Jesus. It is the glory of the Sulamitess to be alone with her King. She exclaims: "My Beloved to me, and I to Him." Thus may we keep our affections so pure and so firmly fixed upon God, that nothing may attach itself to us, and we may attach ourselves to nothing whatsoever.

III. Point.

Reflect what an injury you do your soul, if you allow it to be attached to anything; for if Our Lord should find you in the amiable and holy detachment of the children of God, He will take you into His arms as He did St. Martial in order to bestow upon you the utmost perfection of His love. Blessed, therefore, are detached souls, for Our Lord will clothe them with Himself!

Affections.

Behold, O Lord! a poor, miserable, and insignificant creature before the throne of Thy divine mercy, conjuring Thy paternal goodness to accept these little, though at the same time great, renunciations. Take from me all that clings to my soul, O Lord. I except nothing, tear me from myself. Yes, self, I leave you forever, with no desire to take you back again, unless Our Lord expressly commands me to do so. O desires! O affections! O creatures! O all things! I divest myself entirely of you.

O most sweet Jesus! who didst come naked into the world, and who didst die naked upon the cross, what else hast Thou taught me except to live detached from all things and to sing unceasingly in desire and deed, " Live Jesus, destitute of Father and Mother on the cross! Live His most

CONCLUSION OF THE RETREAT. 173

holy detachment! Live Mary, deprived of her Son at the foot of the cross! Live her most holy renunciation!" Yes, Lord Jesus! may my heart remain entirely divested of all things, even of goods the most spiritual, that Thou mayst be simply and absolutely all things to it.

My soul, proceed henceforth like your divine Model on the path of this world, destitute of all things. From the moment that you find your heart desiring to attach itself to anything whatever, cast all at the feet of Jesus, and there renew the general and particular resolutions of your retreat, so that being clothed with Jesus Christ, you may live in newness of life. *Amen.*

LETTER OF MOTHER JANE FRANCES FRÉMIOT DE CHANTAL

TO THE LATE DEAR AND GOOD MOTHER DE CHÂTEL, FULL OF INSTRUCTION AND OF GREAT UTILITY FOR ANNUAL RETREATS.

My very dear Daughter:

You wish me to tell you what you are to do in your retreat. Ah! my child, you know that I am not capable of saying much to you on this subject. However, to satisfy your kind heart and to condescend to your humility, I shall say that on the first day of retreat, we should not begin to prepare for confession. We should occupy our mind in recollection, keeping our soul tranquil in the presence of God, so that later on, like pure water under the rays of that beautiful Sun, we may clearly see to the bottom. The following day we should make our general examen very sweetly, without eagerness, effort, or curiosity. I would not advise any one to accustom herself to write her annual confession out at length, although those who find it necessary are at liberty to do so. Since the first three or four days should be employed in the purgative way, you may take the first and last meditations of Philothea, or any others like them. On the following day, the Sisters should reflect sweetly on what our meek Saviour has done for love of us, and to redeem us. On the last days, we should make use of a book which treats of the infinite love and eternal riches of this great God; for toward the end of the retreat we must endeavor to strip our heart of all that we know may cling to it. We should place at the feet of Our Lord all those garments, one after the other, supplicating Him to keep them, and to clothe us with Himself, and thus, naked and despoiled before the divine Goodness, we should again cast ourselves into the arms of His providence, leaving to Him the care and government of our whole being. Believe me, my daughter, nothing will be wanting to us. Never should we charge ourselves with any care, desire, affection, or attachment; for, since we have surrendered all to Our Lord, we must permit Him to govern us, while we think only of pleasing Him, either by suffering or by action.

With regard to gaining the indulgence granted to Religious who make a retreat, you should not have the least fear of not gaining it on account of being unable to meditate in detail, nor to meditate with the understanding during the time of prayer. God has given you a method of more simple and intimate intercourse with His goodness. But, my child, behold what you should do: you should read attentively the points upon which you desire to meditate, if you are free to do so, and on reading them, withdraw your mind devoutly to God. This reading will for you take the place of meditation. By it your mind will always receive great benefit; and though it may not be perceptible to you, it will benefit you none the less for that. Having fulfilled your obligation by this reading, later on, during prayer, in your own simple and loving method, I repeat, that you will more than fully satisfy for your meditation, and for this reason: God being infinite in greatness, comprehends all mysteries; consequently, in possessing God, you have the essence of the mystery upon which you meditate. A very spiritual, learned, and virtuous priest, belonging to a religious Order, confirmed me in this opinion. Yes, my very dear daughter, our annual retreat is a most important exercise, and we should try to make it with the utmost devotion and fidelity. I consider that it will be very useful to your daughters, to have read at table the "Exercises of Dom Sens de St. Catharine": for, as His Lordship, that is to say, the blessed Father, who was then alive, remarked to me, it is comprehensive, and the style pleasing, for it is written in that of the saints, flying immortification and detesting the researches of self-love. With regard to meditation, give to your daughters points that are striking, sweet, solid, and touching.

I am, in the divine love, my very dear daughter, your humble and unworthy Sister and servant in Our Lord,

Sister JANE FRANCES FRÉMIOT,
of the Visitation of the Blessed Virgin.

Visitation Convent, Paris, September 18, 1622.

AN EXAMEN ARRANGED BY MOTHER DE CHANTAL,

TO ASSIST IN MAKING AN ANNUAL CONFESSION.

IN the first place, examine yourself on your progress or failing since your last retreat, which is made from year to year. Whether you have not acquired some bad habit, not previously possessed. Cast your eyes on the most ordinary imperfections, temptations, repugnances, and difficulties that you experience in the Rules, Constitutions, and Customs, seeking their source and origin, and discovering them with simplicity. Confess them, and make your renewal with courage and with the resolution to tend courageously to the perfection of your state, by the exercise of the virtues that will be recommended to you in a particular manner.

How do you receive the sacraments? Do you sometimes approach them through routine and imitation, through fear, rather than through devotion? Do you lose their fruit by want of preparation?

In going to confession, are you satisfied to make yourself known as worthy of abjection? If so, you will confess your sins very simply, and in humble terms. You will freely tell your faults and all that can render you more confused and ashamed in presence of the confessor.

Are you faithful in correcting the faults that you confess? Do you make reiterated acts of contrition before going to confession? Having confessed, are you exact in thanking God for this grace, which is, assuredly, very great?

Do you perform some special devotion,

either before or after holy communion? Some practices of virtue for this intention, to keep your mind recollected in memory of this benefit?

Are you distracted soon after receiving holy communion? Are you more humble, sweet, and cordial on the day of communion? For this is the fruit which you should draw from holy communion.

Are you careful to make your intentions at the commencement of each exercise and each important action, offering them to God for His glory and in honor of the Blessed Virgin, or for some other intention?

Are you tepid in prayer and during your practices of piety? Do they weary you? Do you sometimes find the Office long, meditation difficult, spiritual exercises laborious, the returns that you make to God painful? Do you perform your exercises with inattention? Do you resist the lights that God gives you, either to do good or to avoid evil, paying no attention whatever to them, so as to commit your imperfections more freely, and not to undertake the good that is apparent?

How do you go to the Office, and in what manner do you comport yourself while there, at prayer, and during holy Mass? In your examens, do you fail in careful preparation, and in subjecting your mind to follow the teachings that have been given you on this subject, observing what is said of it in the Custom Book?

Are you prompt in rejecting distractions? Do you give rise to them by not keeping strict custody of eyes on certain occasions, or by not keeping your mind recollected during the day, amusing yourself with trifles?

How do you observe the Rule, the Constitutions, and especially your sacred vows?

EXAMEN OF CONSCIENCE.

Do you obey exactly in all things; promptly, without delay; simply, without reply; lovingly, without chagrin; cordially and with a good heart, without murmur; humbly, without criticising and censuring the command? Are you more exact to an honorable command and one of importance, than to those that are trifling and abject?

Do you disobey through negligence, forgetfulness, idleness, or stubbornness, with deliberation, without love for obedience, or for the person who commands, through want of esteem for the command, in things of small importance or otherwise? Accuse yourself carefully on this matter, for it is important.

Have you entertained aversion for the Superioress, causing you to pass unfavorable judgment on her actions and words; that she has spoken or acted through passion, self-interest, particular affection, vanity, and the like? But what would be worse, have you despised her in your heart by not esteeming her orders, her conduct, her judgment, and especially in what relates to the mortifications and corrections which she has given you? This is the true mark by which to know your defects. Have you murmured and complained of her to the Sisters, and even to seculars? In accusing yourself in confession, or in treating of your conscience affairs with a priest, have you made known her defects, or those of others, in order to excuse your own, or under pretext of being well understood? Have you failed in respect to her, by replying to or contradicting her through passion, with audacity, before the Sisters, refusing to obey in order to do your own will, through stubbornness or otherwise? Our obedience should be established on perfect

EXAMEN OF CONSCIENCE.

abnegation of self-will and of our own judgment.

With regard to holy poverty, are you, in effect and affection, a proprietor of something, no matter how small? Have you murmured when something was wanting to you, or when what was given to you was not according to your liking, whether with respect to food, clothing, medicine, bedding, warmth, or some other corporal convenience?

Have you asked for, taken, or given anything without leave? Have you desired, asked for, or retained any unnecessary article, foreseeing that it would be useful to you?

If you have somecharge, have you served the Sisters without choice? Have you willingly given them what was in your care, without any other consideration than that of necessity?

Have you preferred yourself in the distribution of things, no matter what? Our poverty should be stripped of all things.

Our chastity should be angelic. Examine yourself with regard to your imagination, thoughts, desires. Make the examen on this point very simple, though faithful, and accuse yourself with most generous humility and confidence of the faults which you have observed.

EXAMEN WITH REGARD TO SELF.

Well-ordered charity will cause you to care for the purity and advancement of your soul in perfection, and to have very little anxiety for your body. The care of the latter you will leave to your Superioress.

Do you esteem yourself above your neighbor? Do you desire to be esteemed, and for this end, do you boast of yourself in some way or other? Do you pretend to understand spiritual matters, speaking of the interior, saying energetic words to maintain your own opinion, and even at times doing so stubbornly, through vanity and pride? Do you speak advantageously of yourself, of your belongings, of the good which you have done and which you are doing, proposing yourself as an example, under pretext of edifying your neighbor, or of encouraging her to imitate you? Do you speak of your relations, of your possessions in the world, of the honor there rendered you, and even of vain things, such as dances, theatres, dress, promenades, advantageous offers of marriage, and similar follies, amusing yourself by thinking of them, and flattering yourself in the vain belief that you are esteemed and loved? Do you inquire indirectly of what is said of you in your absence? or, rather, when something has been said in your praise, do you endeavor to shorten the conversation, or do you add some jocose words calculated to prolong the discourse and increase the praise, either of yourself or of those whom you love? Do you seek the society of certain persons, not on account of their merit, their virtue, and the respect that you owe them, but through vanity, because they love you, make much of you, and praise you; because it is an honor for you that they know you, that they willingly see you, that they esteem you for your mind, judgment, and conversation?

Are you delighted to speak of the conversations that you have had with some person of distinction, repeating the advice asked of you, and the replies that you have made, when you judge them apropos? All this is very vain.

Do you take pleasure in and amuse yourself by relating your dreams, and expressing your thoughts through vanity, desiring that your hearers interpret them in your favor? Are you sorry to hear others praised, or to know that they are esteemed and loved, judging that all this turns to your disadvantage? Do you try to lessen the praise bestowed upon them, either by your words or by your silence, or what would be still worse, by relating their defects through jealousy, pride, envy, fearing not to be loved, esteemed, and preferred?

Do you resent humiliations and corrections? Do you murmur in thought or word against them? Have you diminished your affection or conceived some aversion and want of confidence toward those who have been instrumental in correcting you, or who have warned you of your faults? Are you grieved to be employed in things low and vile? Are you disgusted with having

EXAMEN OF CONSCIENCE.

trifling employments, preferring and occupying yourself more assiduously in things that are high and honorable, desiring the first offices under any pretext whatever? This is very injurious, and an assured mark of little virtue.

Do you yield to impatience in trifles? Are you subject to feelings of anger? Do you give expression to them in word or action? or do you overcome yourself?

Are the faults you commit owing to impulse, inadvertence, or for a reason long and deliberately entertained with regard to the matter under consideration? Do you perform actions through spite upon the slightest contradictions? Are the words that you use to gratify your resentment sharp, scolding, proud, cold, dry, sarcastic, intended to annoy the person who has saddened you, or are they revengeful, showing your passion? Do you look coldly at

EXAMEN OF CONSCIENCE.

her, reply to her in monosyllables, or pretend not to hear her, and similar defects?

Have you acquiesced in the will of seculars, and treated them with human respect, through fear of displeasing them? Have you remained away from the Office and the other exercises without necessity, in order to entertain them with vain and frivolous subjects? Have you listened long to unnecessary news and to useless things without interrupting them, through the pleasure that you take in them. Do you, although seeing their vanity, laugh at their folly, and commit acts of levity and worldliness, thus encouraging them to become too familiar toward you? Being too free with them leads to evil, and to the detriment of your perfection.

Do you multiply words? Do you use exaggerated expressions in order needlessly to testify your affection? Do you praise your friends, telling them in unrestrained terms that they are esteemed, that they are preferred, that they are spoken well of in their absence, that they are much thought of, and that people wish to see them? On the other hand, are you at times too cold, not testifying the devout, sweet, and holy cordiality of your Institute?

Do you tell trifling falsehoods through precipitation or inadvertence, to excuse yourself, to embellish your conversation? Do you disguise the truth, concealing under a specious pretext your intentions in slight and indifferent matters and for various motives? Do you often do this, especially in giving an account of your interior? or what would be still worse, does this happen in confession?

Do you resort to some artifice to show that you are not well, or that you have need of something, without saying so frankly

EXAMEN OF CONSCIENCE. 193

and asking for it, for fear of being considered tender and immortified?

Do you pretend to have more regret for your faults than you actually entertain in your heart? You will know this, if you are as contrite for them when you have recognized them and when no one but yourself has seen them, as when you tell them or are corrected for them. Do the tears that you shed, or the exaggerated words that you use, proceed from pride, which is displeased that we are known to be guilty, and pleased to have it known that we ourselves recognize our faults, and have a bad opinion of ourselves, and of all that we do?

Do you make vain reflections, when obliged to give an account of the good you have done, of the extraordinary graces that God has given you in prayer, speaking only in monosyllables and pretending to be ashamed while telling your faults? All that is pride, which makes you fear that others will believe that you make much account of these matters, and that is a great defect in simplicity. Do you conceal your faults, especially when they are abject, saying many useless words to prove the necessity that caused you to commit them?

Do you testify more appearance of pain than you feel when you are treated as a sick person, or when on some occasion you are preferred to others? The refusal that you make of viands, of some convenience, of some service, does it show vain courage and duplicity, rather than a desire of suffering the want or the inconvenience? You will know this, if your heart remains tranquil in suffering, and if you do not amuse yourself by thinking of what is wanting to you.

Do you feign to refuse some amelioration through virtue, when, in truth, you

EXAMEN OF CONSCIENCE.

do so through immortification, the thing proposed not being agreeable to you? All this is hypocrisy and vanity. Do you play the courageous before others, when they sympathize with you about your pains and sufferings, while all the time you are anxious to discover the cause of your illness, and to seek for remedies even the most expensive?

Are you troubled when you are not thought so ill as you really are, or as you appear to be, or when similar neglects occur? Do you note even your most trifling sufferings?

Do you say words through a movement of sensuality, cunningly making known what you like and desire, so that it may be given you?

Are you fastidious in eating, whether in health or in sickness, delicate and hard to please, wishing only what is to your taste, although it may be injurious to your health?

Do you complain of not being well treated, and that your Superiors are not anxious to give you what your appetite requires, when you are ill? When the food is to your taste, do you take too much, although it may be only fruit and water? Do you worry about the length of the nights, your sufferings, and the necessary remedies? Do you obey the infirmarian or the doctor with regret, doing what they order with chagrin and complaint?

See, in fine, how you exercise yourself in the mortification of your heart, which is practised by renouncing self-will, self-judgment, the passions and inclinations, submitting in all things, condescending cheerfully to the will of others.

EXAMEN OF THE STATE OF THE SOUL TOWARD OUR NEIGHBOR.

Do you love every one cordially for the love of God, as well in particular as in general?

If you love your neighbor or the Sisters who are disagreeable as much as those whose qualities naturally please you, your love is good; if you love them less, it is imperfect, and frequently prejudicial. Examine whether you have an upright heart in their regard, whether you do them no harm, whether you pray as fervently for them as for those that please you. Do you fail in support toward your neighbor, either with regard to her corporal or spiritual infirmities? Do you judge rashly of her actions, particularly of the actions of her whom you do not love?

Are you addicted to suspicions on the

slightest provocation? Do you criticise your neighbor's intentions, her reasons, according to your own fancy, and to her disadvantage, sometimes through passion, again through vanity, pretending to a discernment of character and natural inclinations, etc.? Do you boast of the judgment you have formed, and sometimes assert it as true, from the experience you have had yourself of similar faults?

Do you without real necessity speak of her sins, her imperfections? Do you relate her bad humors, pitying her, but through passion and with exaggeration, in order to gratify your aversion for her, or to avenge some slight received from her?

Have you experienced a feeling of joy, when those from whom you have received some contradiction have been mortified? That is a spirit of revenge. Have you repeated some trifling anecdote to the Sisters,

EXAMEN OF CONSCIENCE. 199

that they may know what they who have displeased you have done? Examine whether you have not directly told them of it from the same motive, whether you have not exaggerated the fault, or misinterpreted it to your own advantage. That would be a grievous fault against charity.

Have you despised your Sisters in thought or in deed on account of their mind, their manner, their countenance, throwing out little hints with regard to their origin, that they are beneath you? That would be a serious fault, insupportable vanity. If you yourself are of low extraction, have you in your heart or in your actions preferred yourself to others? Have you made use of disagreeable, carping, acrimonious words, which might offend and displease them, and this even to seculars, contesting and replying with impatience, arrogantly maintaining your own opinion, even in small matters? That would be a great and very disedifying fault.

Have you disputed imperiously, despising the judgment and advice of those with whom you spoke? Have you taken pleasure in acting in this manner, being determined to quarrel or to give offence? Have you long entertained such a thought? That is all very bad.

Are you inclined to envy, which rouses satisfaction in your heart when they whom you see esteemed commit faults, and when these faults are noticed? Do you find it difficult to allow them to be excused or consoled in anything? Examine your heart thoroughly on this subject, and acknowledge your transgressions as frankly and simply as possible. If there is anything that worries you,—doubt, temptation or difficulty—ask to be enlightened thereon.

This examen contains special direction,

EXAMEN OF CONSCIENCE. 201

and gives not only a method for confession, but, moreover, one for the practice of the virtues. It is very useful once a year to see thoroughly the state of the soul, although one is not obliged to accuse herself so minutely of all these matters unless she wishes to do so. A traveller should discover the bad road to avoid it, and the good one to follow it. Self-love has spread its snares throughout the whole course of the spiritual life, so that it is impossible to escape it, unless, as says the glorious St. Anthony, by passing under it, we humble ourselves profoundly, examine ourselves seriously, accuse ourselves sincerely, and, in short, work out our salvation with a holy trembling, a chaste and filial fear, which will make us walk in simplicity of heart, in holiness, in justice, and in truth before God. May the divine goodness grant us the grace to accomplish this undertaking, through the intercession of His most pure Mother, His holy foster-father, St. Joseph, and of the holy Founder, St. Francis de Sales.

Printed in Great Britain
by Amazon

42940668R00116